FATH

and the

PENNINE WAY

MARK RICHARDS

Dedication

This must be the easiest dedication any author has ever written. Thanks, Alex: thanks for coming with me, thanks for getting me through – especially on Wednesday! But above all, thanks for being my son.

"Do you want to come for a walk with me?"

"With Pepper? I'm busy..."

"No, not with the dog. Further than that. The Pennine Way. 5 days: 80 miles. In the summer holidays."

There, I've said it. Ah well, it was a nice idea.

There are a thousand reasons why he'll say no.

Alex looks at me. He shrugs. "Sure," he says. "Why not?"

Yes, I wanted a physical challenge: yes, I was undoubtedly getting older and yes, I wanted to test myself. But it went deeper than that. There was another reason: one I was keeping to myself. I wanted to prove something: I wanted to prove I was alive.

But 17 year old boys are not big on emotional speeches. Especially from their dad. So I said, "Thanks." And added, "Thanks for coming with me. Thanks for giving me the chance to do this. I'm really grateful. And I love you."

"You're welcome," my son said. And he started walking up the hill towards Malham Cove – and five days with his dad.

Whether Pen y Ghent was a hill or a mountain the path did go straight up the side. I looked up again. My fear of heights stirred: the Dementors liked what they saw. I could feel them flexing their muscles. But Alex was right. There was only one way to reach the B&B, and that way was straight up.

I don't have a tattoo. But I was beginning to see the attraction of *Hawes to Tan Hill 3.8.16.* Possibly on my forehead...

What were we going to lose? An hour? An hour and a half? I squelched along the path. My boots were soaking. My socks were soaking. My feet were soaking. My shorts. Even my underpants. What a bloody cock-up.

I glanced behind me. Alex was following me. Maybe a hundred yards behind me. 4½ days of getting on perfectly, of the best father/son time of my life. And we blow it on the last day.

Through Birkdale and up towards Moss Shop, through something marked 'danger area' on the map. "What's that red flag, Dad?"

"It's nothing. Just means we're in the middle of a live firing range, that's all."

As we walk up the hill Alex starts to pull away from me. I'd imagined us walking into Dufton together, but he's in front and that seems right. I hang back and reflect on everything he's given me over the five days. Everything the Pennine Way has given me...

Copyright

Part 1: The Invitation
Prologue. And a warning...

If you're a serious walker with years of experience, a well-worn backpack and a healthy collection of knee supports it's probably best if you look away now. For the sake of your sanity, you shouldn't buy – or read – this book.

You'll say that I hadn't done my homework. That I wasn't remotely prepared for the Pennine Way.

You'll scoff and shake your head at my lack of preparation: you'll point out that I didn't take the right clothing or the right equipment.

And you'd be right.

But I wasn't a serious walker. I wasn't even a walker.

I was a writer. Someone who spent his working life bent over a keyboard: but someone who, in February 2016, suddenly decided he wanted a physical challenge before he was too old for a physical challenge.

Even more importantly, I'm a dad. And I was a dad who wanted to spend some time with his son while he wanted to spend some time with me: some precious father/son time before he went to university and things were never quite the same again.

When I asked Alex if he wanted to come with me the furthest I'd walked was four miles, on a sunny afternoon with the dog.

So no, I wasn't prepared and no, I hadn't done my homework. In the same way that people say they climbed Everest 'because it was there,' I asked Alex to come on the Pennine Way because I'd heard of it. And five days and my original estimate of 80 miles sounded about right for a physical challenge: and it sounded about as much time as a 17 year old boy would want to spend with his dad in the summer holidays.

This isn't a guide book – although you could probably use it as one. At the end you'll find a section on the nuts and bolts of the walk: the stats, what I'd do differently, how we had our bags moved and – worryingly – 'Things I learned about my dad on the Pennine Way...' All the information you need to follow in our footsteps is there.

But principally, this is a story – and you should read it as such. It's a story about the challenges we faced and the experiences we shared. It's a buddy movie where the buddy was my son. It's a road trip on foot. It's what we discovered about ourselves – and about each other. And it's the story of how I came to walk a mile in my underpants...

And for some of you – maybe with a small child asleep next to you, or a teenager who won't be a teenager for much longer – I hope that one day the book will also be an inspiration.

The Pennine Way

Let's start with some history...

The initial suggestion for the Pennine Way came from journalist and rambler Tom Stephenson, who'd been inspired by similar 'national trails' in the USA. He first floated the idea in the *Daily Herald* in 1935. The final section of the route was eventually declared open 30 years later – making the Pennine Way 51 years old when Alex and I stepped out of the River House Bed & Breakfast on August 1st 2016 and started walking.

It now runs from Edale, in the North Derbyshire Peak District, through the Yorkshire Dales and the Northumberland National Park and ends – after 267 miles – at Kirk Yetholm, just over the Scottish border.

The Pennine Way isn't the longest of the UK's national trails, but – according to the Ramblers' Association, who should know about these things – it is 'one of the country's toughest.' In February 2016 I *didn't* know that...

The Invitation

It was a Sunday afternoon at the end of February. *Alex,* I texted, *can you come downstairs? I want to ask you a question.*

Why am I doing this? He's 17: he's not going to say 'yes.' And what the hell am I going to do if he *does* say 'yes?' How will I get out of it?

What I'm going to suggest to my son is ludicrous: so far outside my comfort zone that it's out of sight. So far beyond anything I've ever done in my life that, bluntly, I've no real idea of *what* I'm suggesting. But I've sent the text – and here he is.

"What is it?"

"I've a question to ask you..."

"I know. I read the text."

"Do you want to come for a walk with me?"

"With Pepper? I'm busy..."

"No, not with the dog. Further than that. The Pennine Way. 5 days: 80 miles. In the summer holidays."

There, I've said it. Ah well, it was a nice idea.

Yeah, right, Dad. Like you could walk 80 miles.

I'm going to get a summer job. I'll be working all the time.

Five days? Just the two of us? I'm not sure that'll work, Dad.

There are a thousand reasons why he'll say no.

Alex looks at me. He shrugs. "Sure," he says. "Why not?"

"Why?" Beverley, my wife, is sitting across the table. The voice of reason and logic. She's been silent so far. I hadn't told her what I was planning. She'll talk me out of it.

"Because I want a physical challenge. I want to test myself. Do something I've never done before. And I need to do it before my left knee decides the only thing it's good for is a waiting list. And I want to spend some time with my son..."

As I say, the voice of reason and logic.

Don't be ridiculous. All you do is walk the dog on the cliff top. Preferably on a sunny day. You're a writer. You spend your days slumped over your desk. You eat too much cheese. Drink too much red wine.

"It's a brilliant idea," she says.

Three words from my son: four from my wife. That's all it takes.

"Are you sure?" I ask Alex.

He sighs and looks at me. Old age. Everything needs repeating these days. "Sure. I like walking with you." He pauses – and turns to what's *really* important. "What time's dinner?"

"Six," I say. And he disappears back to his bedroom, leaving me stunned. And committed – to five days on the Pennine Way.

I'd done some research: my plan was to start in Malham, just north of Skipton in the Yorkshire Dales, and finish in Dufton – 13 miles from Carlisle, in Cumbria. But at that moment the words 'Malham,' 'Dufton' and 'Pennine Way' were just that – words. Mordor, Middle Earth and the Forbidden Forest were more real to me.

I didn't even know where the idea had come from.

"Dad?" Alex was back. And with a crucial question.

"Where are we going to sleep?"

"In B&Bs. Bed and breakfasts. You know that tents have never been one of my strong points."

"Will we have separate rooms?" And there it was, the deal-breaker. No self-respecting 17 year old would share a room with his dad for five days. No chance.

"I don't think we can. Not if we're staying in B&Bs. Two rooms would be too expensive. Sharing a room is the price you pay for a full English every morning."

"OK, that's fine." And he went back upstairs.

Leaving his dad to go online and look at pictures of hills. And more hills...

Why?

A day later I was walking along the beach: the South Bay at Scarborough. It was lunchtime: bananas, an apple and mineral water were waiting in the office. Satan – disguised as my previous life, a cheese and tomato sandwich, packet of crisps and a Coke – was firmly behind me. Unlike the wind, which was firmly in front of me. And straight from Siberia.

I was worrying. Not about the wind: I was worrying about why I was doing this – and whether I *could* do it.

After Alex had gone back to his bedroom I'd read the website of someone who knew what he was talking about. 'You can expect to go at 2mph on the Pennine Way.'

So 16 miles a day meant eight hours of walking. A whole new meaning for 9-to-5. I gritted my teeth, pulled my coat around me and marched resolutely onwards.

Thirty minutes later I was back at my desk. I didn't 'slump over my desk:' instead I drank my water, ate the fruit as slowly as a starving man could eat fruit, and asked myself some questions.

Why was I doing this?

The answer I'd given my wife – "I want to do a physical challenge before my left knee decides the only thing it's good for is a waiting list" – was a nice soundbite. And it was fine for public consumption. Yes, I wanted a physical challenge: yes, I was undoubtedly getting older and yes, I wanted to test myself. But it went deeper than that.

There was another reason: one I was keeping to myself.

I wanted to prove something: I wanted to prove I was alive.

Ten years ago – completely out of the blue – I was critically ill. I spent four days in intensive care. At one point the phrase 'touch and go' was being used. I don't want to interrupt the flow of the story with all the details, but if you want to know what 'touch and go' really meant – and why I had something to prove to myself – there is a chapter at the back of the book.

When I came out of hospital I set myself a simple target: walk to the lamppost nearest our house. I've just done it now – it's exactly 200 steps, not quite 200 yards.

In my time I had run half-marathons. But on a Tuesday morning in April 2006 I couldn't walk to the nearest lamppost.

I'd asked my eldest son, Dan, to come with me. He was 12 at the time.

"Where are we going, Dad?"

"Up to the first lamppost. Just up the road. I'll be fine. But just in case..."

I was 50 or 60 yards away when I realised I wasn't going to get there. "Hang on, Dan. I can't do this. Help me back to the house."

I watched the emotions chase each other across his face. Confusion. Then worry, sadness, pity. And finally, disappointment.

In retrospect, not something a 12 year old should have experienced: not my finest piece of parenting. And not expressions I wanted to see on my son's face.

That moment – the moment I saw my son realise his dad was all too mortal – had haunted me for ten years. 80 miles in five days seemed a reasonable way of laying the ghost to rest.

Was I physically fit enough?

Right there and then the answer was 'no.' My wife was right. Thanks to wine and cheese and the fruit of the bacon sandwich tree I was overweight. An hour with the dog was my limit. Now I was proposing to walk 8 hours a day for five consecutive days on 'one of the country's toughest' national trails...

Yes, I'd lost some weight since Beverley gave me a Fitbit for Christmas. But two-thirds of my clothes were still out of bounds when I opened the wardrobe door.

And what about my left knee? Last time I'd walked up the cliff from the beach it had stopped working. *Sorry, mate. I'm getting old. I'm having five minutes off.* And my right hamstring: 11 or 12 years since I foolishly challenged my daughter to a race up a sand dune and had to be helped back to the car by my sniggering children. I still felt the twinges. Even if the spirit was willing, a large percentage of the flesh was decidedly weak.

Why the Pennine Way?

Because I'd read about it. Maybe I'd seen it on *Countryfile*. I honestly don't know. It was the only walk I'd heard of and – when I looked – there was plenty of information on Google.

In retrospect we could have done 80 miles on the Coast to Coast walk and finished at Robin Hood's Bay, 15 miles from home. Bev could have popped some jacket potatoes in the oven and driven across the Moors to collect us – instead of a three hour cross country trek to the outskirts of Carlisle. (She hasn't realised that yet: keep it to yourself, will you?)

How much did I know about walking?

If you're ridiculously old you'll have heard of Len Shackleton, the 'Clown Prince of Football.' Len played for Newcastle and Sunderland just after the Second World War. In his autobiography he famously had a chapter called 'The Average Director's Knowledge of Football.' It consisted of a single blank page.

I was tempted to follow suit: 'My Knowledge of Walking on February 28th.'

Maybe I was ahead of Len's average director – but only just. I'd passed plenty of serious walkers when I'd been out with the dog. I knew they had boots and backpacks and determined faces. A lot of them seemed to be held together with support bandages. But that was it. Oh, and I'd once taken a girlfriend to the Lake District for the weekend. But definitely not for the walking.

And what about Alex?

Bluntly, would we still be friends at the end of five days?

When the children were younger we'd often rent a cottage for holidays. There was one in Northumberland we went back to three or four times: the Old Country Chapel in Halton Lea Gate, roughly halfway between Hexham and Carlisle.

One day – when his brother and sister were exhausted from damming up the local stream – I asked Alex if he wanted to come for a walk with me. He was seven or eight. We walked down the lane and then turned right, up onto the hills. We must have been close to – maybe even on – the section of the Pennine Way that runs from Knarsdale to Greenhead.

We were out for two hours. Just a boy and his dad, walking through the countryside, talking as they went.

And that was the start of it. Alex carried on walking with me: long, rambling walks with the dog, talking about life, history, growing-up, school, friends, politics, philosophy and – when he was old enough – the character defects of his teachers...

Those walks were some of my happiest moments as a dad.

We discussed serious questions. Does God exist? (A tough one: big brother Dan is firmly in the Big Bang camp. Alex has a much more open mind...) Is space infinite? ("It can't be can it, Dad? If space is infinite there's a planet where you're a rock star...")

We talked about the future; about careers; about what sort of father he'd be one day. And we talked openly. What had I got wrong? What would he do differently when he was a dad?

We talked about his relationships with girls...

No, we didn't. Don't be ridiculous. However close you are to your son, at 17 some things are *way* off limits

But my relationship with Alex was infinitely precious to me. Taking a risk with my health was one thing: risking my relationship with my son was entirely different.

The Gory Details

There's no point writing a book like this unless you're totally honest – especially about your own failings. So here we go.

Enough of the 'nowhere near fit enough' and 'slightly overweight' nonsense.

You want the truth; the gory details; the full horror story. It's time for Tubby Lardpants to 'fess up…

On Saturday, December 5th 2015 I opened a new file in Evernote. It was called 'Sort Myself Out.'

I weighed 105.4kg. If you're in the UK and you still work in old money that's 16st 8lbs. If you're in the US, it's 232lbs. I won't tell you what my body fat percentage was – you might be eating your breakfast.

By Christmas Day Lardpants was down to 102.8kg. At which point Beverley gave me a Fitbit. It's no understatement to say that it changed my life.

The Fitbit's demands were simple. Walk 10,000 steps a day. 'What?' I thought at the time. 'How in God's name do you walk 10,000 steps a day?' Stories filtered through of a doctor friend who was doing 17,000 steps a day – apparently by pacing the hospital corridors in between screwing patients back together.

My first day with the Fitbit produced 3,874 steps. 17,000? I dismissed it as the stuff of fantasy: something only a hollow-cheeked fanatic could achieve.

But gradually I made some changes. I applied the law of marginal gains. British cycling was awash with gold medals thanks to Dave Brailsford's concept of 'marginal gains' – the cumulative sum of lots of very small improvements. Why couldn't I be awash with jeans that fitted again?

So I parked at the far end of the car park; made a couple of detours on the way to the office; stopped walking to the sandwich shop at lunchtime and walked along the beach instead.

And one day it happened. I was walking past Scarborough's Art Gallery and my Fitbit suddenly started buzzing and vibrating. It was having an orgasm right there on my wrist. I'd done it. 10,000 steps. Next stop the hospital corridor...

By the time Alex said 'yes' at the end of February I was 96.5kg (15st 3lbs or 213lbs) – and managing my 10,000 steps four or five days a week.

But I still wasn't a walker. I'd lost 19lbs by the simple method of turning right for the beach instead of left for the sandwich shop. I was walking for 25-30 minutes a day, doing maybe 1½ miles in jeans and trainers I kept at the office.

And with 16 weeks to go, 'nowhere near fit enough' still applied. But walking was my only option. See above: left knee, right hamstring – running was out of the question. And I definitely didn't want to join the legions of middle aged men who slipped erotically into some Lycra, forgot to look in the mirror and then clambered onto a bike.

But I was beginning to realise that Scarborough beach – beautiful as it was in the spring sunshine – bore little resemblance to Pen y Ghent and Great Shunner Fell. I'd looked at a map and dredged up what I remembered from Mad Mick Lawson's Geography lessons: "Contour lines that are close together mean a steep hill, you stupid boy."

Strolling along the beach fantasising about summer and wearing my shorts might be working for my waistline: it wasn't preparing me for the Pennine Way.

The choice was simple: do some proper training or have another – rather more painful – conversation with my son. Maybe the answer was to do some reconnaissance: see exactly what I'd let myself in for. Besides, we had a wedding anniversary to celebrate.

I drank my water, ate yet another damn banana and Googled 'best B&B in the Dales.'

It was time to meet the enemy...

"I've forgotten the map..."

We stayed at the Priory Guesthouse in Middleham. If you want to Google the room and imagine my wife lazing in the copper bath looking at the boyhood home of Richard III it was Castle View. Meanwhile I was lazing by the window, watching Mark Johnston's string of impossibly beautiful racehorses clip-clop their way up the main street to the gallops.

We lingered over poached eggs and bacon. When someone else has cooked breakfast I can linger for a long time, especially when toast and fresh coffee are beating a regular path to our table.

But duty – and hills – were calling.

We were on holiday. Sightseeing was allowed: so we detoured to Aysgarth Falls. For the film buffs among you, it's where Kevin Costner, *Prince of Thieves*, refused to give way to John Little and disappeared into the water.

And then it was Hawes – and my first encounter with the Pennine Way.

"We'll be here on the Tuesday night," I said. "Wednesday is Hawes to the Tan Hill Inn." How remarkably simple it sounded in the spring sunshine...

We went for coffee: the Herriot Gallery. And they did B&B. "You may as well book it now," Bev said. I paid the £20 deposit, booked a twin room for Tuesday August 2nd and put another tick in the commitment column.

I would have lingered over the mid-morning coffee as well, but my wife was having none of it. "Come on," she said. "We're not here to drink coffee. Where's the Ordnance Survey map?"

"Ah..." I'd had that nagging, left-something-behind feeling all morning. "I've left it in the bedroom."

My wife sighed the sigh of someone who's brought up three children and was now dealing with a fourth. "Thank goodness you'll be going with a grown up."

So we bought another map and walked back to the car. "We're going up there," I said, pointing at a hill in front of us. The top of it was lost in low cloud. What I could see looked impossibly steep. "Great Shunner Fell..."

But first some light entertainment courtesy of the BBC. We drove past Simonstone Hall. "Look," I said. "Isn't that where Jeremy Clarkson thumped the producer? Twenty years from now that'll be worth a blue plaque."

"They've already got one. It was on the news."

Was there nothing the woman didn't know? I grudgingly bowed to my wife's superior knowledge of current affairs and dropped down a gear as the climb became ominously steeper.

"There," I said as I found a lay-by and pulled over. "Finally reached the top."

"You probably need to start saying 'summit' now..."

We climbed out of the car and stood on the side of the road. The low cloud had cleared – and the view was breathtaking. Endless hills stretched in front of us, a stream ran along the bottom of the valley.

It was breathtaking and beautiful. But bleak.

"What is it?" Bev asked.

"I'm feeling... I'm realising... What we're going to do. I think 'daunted' is the word. The hills go on for ever. They're infinite..."

"And it's exposed."

"That's one thing we *don't* need to worry about," I said confidently. "We're going in the first week of August remember."

"So there you are. All you need to do is put one foot in front of the other."

But for eight hours? For five consecutive days?

Ten minutes later we dropped down into Keld. "Four miles to Tan Hill," I said. "Lunchtime. All this walking has made me hungry."

"Thinking about walking," my wife said gently.

The sign pointed to Tan Hill. Obediently, I turned the corner. And everyone who's driven a car will have known that moment. A country road you haven't been on before: you turn a corner and suddenly the road rears up in front of you. Instantly you're in first gear desperately trying to remember how to do a hill start. "Quite steep," my wife said. "Welcome to the Yorkshire Dales, darling."

And if Great Shunner Fell had been bleak the road to the Tan Hill Inn was even bleaker.

Dating back to the 17th Century and once used as a hostel by workers digging coal pits, the Tan Hill Inn is now the highest pub in the country at 1,732ft. Just to reassure me that it was never exposed to any bad weather there was a snowplough in the car park.

I stood outside the pub and gazed north. The hills seemed to stretch to Scotland. There was a road in the distance, the sun reflecting off the cars. "The A66," I said. "We'll cross that on Thursday."

"The border with County Durham, darling. Into foreign lands..."

"I'll remember my passport," I said. "How far do you think it is? Two miles? Four miles? It's hard to judge distances when all you can see is hills."

"That's why you have a map, darling. When you remember to bring it."

Game, set and match to the wife. We went inside for lunch.

Face to Face with Real Walking

I'd come back from Middleham feeling – yes, daunted had been the right word – but more focused. I was still walking along the beach but now I was gradually increasing my mileage and going out of my way to walk uphill. The two days in the Dales had frightened me: but they'd inspired me as well. "Come on," I said to Pepper, a slightly baffled Springer Spaniel, and ran up another flight of stairs between the beach huts.

By mid-May – with ten weeks to go – the spring sunshine had dried out the cliff top: it was time for some serious training to start.

"Don't overdo it," Beverley said.

"Don't worry, I'm going to do five miles at 18 minute mile pace. And I'm starting at Burniston Rocks and going north."

"What? On the cliff top?"

"Less of the 'cliff top.' It's the Cleveland Way now."

"Well, like I say. Don't overdo it."

"I'll be fine. It's flat. What does Alex always tell me? 'There are no hills on the cliff top.'"

"You mean the Cleveland Way, darling..."

An hour later I dragged myself to the top of yet another endless flight of stone steps and realised I'd finally come face to face with real walking. Walkmeter – the simplest walking app I could find for my iPhone – told me I'd done 2½ miles at a depressing 21 minutes per mile. And I'd laughed when someone said 2mph was reasonable for the Pennine Way.

I'd started at the car park where I used to take the children down to the rocks: 'Crook Ness,' according to the OS map. Then I walked north past Long Nab and Hundale Scar and Rodger Trod. 'Less of the cliff top' was right: those were proper walking names...

My 'flat' five miles ended up as 5.16 miles in an hour and 40 minutes. Just over 3mph. But that was without a backpack. Without a break for lunch.

"Well you did it," Beverley said.

"Yes, I did." And I was proud of myself. But now I was exhausted. To put it bluntly, I was knackered. And my left knee hurt – not a good sign after five miles. Ten weeks from now I had to walk three times as far: for five days in a row.

"You're not having doubts are you?"

"No, no, not at all," I said – and somewhere close by a lie detector went into overdrive.

But let's have the glass half-full: that Sunday morning had taught me some valuable lessons...

That training for the Pennine Way by walking along the beach – fantasising about sunny weather and my shorts – was like training for an all-you-can-eat challenge by ordering a mixed leaf salad. Nice to look at but useless. From now on it had to be hills and more hills.

There's a reason why people recommend walking boots with ankle supports. University accommodation bills from Dan and our daughter, Ellie, may have pushed my boots down the priority list: 5 miles in 100 minutes just pushed them back up it. My walking shoes – Mountain Warehouse, thirty quid – had been fine so far, but I clearly needed an upgrade.

And the final lesson: walking along the Cleveland Way mentally framing your next jaw-droppingly wonderful photograph is fine. Just remember not to fall over a tree-stump while you're doing it...

There was something else as well. As I stood on the cliffs, high above Hayburn Wyke, gazing south to Flamborough Head and north towards Robin Hood's Bay, watching a snowy owl make one last, lazy reconnaissance flight over a field, I'd realised something very simple.

I'd fallen in love with walking.

Standing there, the early morning sun glinting off the North Sea, I realised how much I loved the solitude and the stillness: the time to reflect: the views, the emptiness – and the sheer joy of being outside and active while the rest of the world was stumbling downstairs to breakfast.

"How was it, Dad?" Alex asked me over dinner that night.

"Different," I said. "Challenging. Slippery. Hilly."

"I've told you. There aren't any hills on the cliff top."

"You can forget the words 'cliff top.' I've already told your mother: it's the Cleveland Way to us serious walkers."

"Call it what you like. It doesn't have any hills."

Thus spoke the boy who'd done a Duke of Edinburgh expedition in the Lake District. And I knew he was right. Even as I'd hauled myself to the top of the stone steps I'd known they were nothing compared to the hills I'd seen on the road to Tan Hill. I'd spent the afternoon pushing the thought out of my mind.

"Well, hills or no hills," I said, "It's too late to change our minds now. I've booked all the B&Bs, paid the deposits."

"Great. I'm really looking forward to it," he said, casually ratcheting the pressure up another notch.

"Have you got everything you need?" Beverley asked.

"Pretty much," I said. "Apart from a pair of boots for both of us. And I need some walking trousers – those sexy ones that unzip and turn into shorts – socks, waterproof trousers. And a waterproof jacket, I suppose."

"So in reality you haven't got anything?"

"No," I was forced to admit.

"You'll need a hat as well, Dad," Alex said.

"What for?"

"In case it rains."

"How many times? We're going in the first week of August. Besides, I look like a knob in a hat." I turned to my wife. "Tell him I don't need a hat."

"Your father's right, darling. By the end of day five he'll be wearing a red t-shirt, those yellow shorts he bought because he knew they'd annoy me, blue socks and muddy boots. He'll look like a Romanian flag that's been dragged through a field. Trust me, sweetheart, we've been married for 23 years. Your father doesn't need a hat to look like a knob."

The Sum of All my Fears

Yes, I'd learned some valuable lessons on that Sunday morning. More significantly, I'd also come face to face with my fears.

Walking along the beach the day after asking Alex if he'd come with me I'd wondered if my body was up to it. I'd wondered if our relationship would survive the five days.

But that had been theory.

My first five miles of proper walking had turned it into reality. The word had been made flesh – and weak flesh at that. If my knee was hurting after five miles, what would it be like after 75 miles?

Sorry, Alex, I need a rest. Long sigh. *Not another one, Dad. Which part of your body has fallen off now?*

And I had a couple of new opponents to contend with as well...

I'd discovered I was frightened of walking down slippery stone steps. Yes, it was early in the morning; yes, there'd been some rain overnight. But had I really needed to be so careful? Did I really need to walk down the steps like an arthritic old man tip-toeing through a minefield?

Yes, I did. As the A&E department will testify, I have a long and spectacular record of falling over.

"I'll just jump over this wall." Ripped my suit, tore my ankle ligaments.

"Watch, Dan. You put the ball between your feet and flick it up like this." Trod on the football as I landed, tore the other ankle ligaments.

And most spectacularly of all, slipped on the ice coming out of a school parents' evening: lying flat on my back on the school drive in front of an audience of parents and teenage children. Dan – 17 at the time – was rushed to hospital with very-nearly-fatal embarrassment. So maybe I was right to file a wet, well-worn flight of stone steps under 'lethal weapons.'

But how could I walk on the Pennine Way if I was frightened of walking downhill? Clearly, I had to walk up Pen y Ghent: equally clearly I had to come down the other side.

Was I the only walker frightened of going downhill? Not according to Google. I typed in *fear of walking downhill.* 520,000 results – and what do you know, it has a sexy Latin name: Bathmophobia. 'A fear of stairs or steep slopes.' Feeling reassured – and significantly more cheerful – I checked to see if I shared the condition with anyone famous.

Well, well. Donald J. Trump...

And there was something else. My fear of heights: acrophobia – from the Greek word 'akron', meaning peak, summit or edge. As I'd stood on the cliffs above the Hayburn Wyke – 300 feet above sea-level and two steps from the edge – it had swirled around me like Harry Potter's Dementors. Let's just hope the 2,277 feet to the top of Pen y Ghent was on a gentle and well-trodden path.

With ten weeks to go that was the sum of my fears: two phobias, work still to do on my fitness, a dodgy knee and a relationship with my son to preserve.

I wasn't sure how much of this to share with Alex. I'm not a dad who's afraid to show his feelings – and it's a very long time since my children saw me as some sort of Superman.

But I didn't want my son thinking he'd signed up to be walking coach, nursemaid and psychologist...

Meeting my Ancestor

Rewind two months to a Sunday at the end of March. I was halfway between Scarborough and Whitby, parked on a long abandoned Moors road. My mission – which my wife told me I'd accepted – was to collect Alex from his Duke of Edinburgh practice expedition. Dropped off on Saturday morning, to be collected on a wet Sunday afternoon.

I gazed out of the car window. Was the drizzle light enough to get out and finish my 10,000 steps? Oh, sod it. I didn't have a choice. Beverley was making stew and dumplings and opening the red wine. A human sacrifice was required. I resigned myself to getting wet, underlined 'waterproof coat' on my mental still-to-buy list and opened the car door. I pulled my hood up and headed for the North York Moors. I only needed to do 10 minutes: Alex wouldn't be back for a while.

"Dad!" I hadn't taken ten steps when I heard his voice. There he was, coming over the hill, an orange pack on his back. An *enormous* orange pack on his back. How had he possibly carried that for two days?

"Hi. How are you doing?"

"Yeah, I'm good. What's for dinner?"

If that's the first question your teenage soon asks after two days on the North York Moors then you know he's OK. Not something you could say for some of the others. They plodded slowly back to their parents like the mud-spattered stragglers in the

Grand National. Several mothers turned their eyes to the heavens and mentally resigned themselves to Sunday night with the washing machine.

"Tough?" I asked.

"In parts. Come on," he said. "I'm starving."

And now, two months later, we were back in the very same place. Our first official father/son training session. The March drizzle had given way to a beautiful early-June morning. Just as well, because the Pennine Way was eight weeks away and my training schedule demanded nine miles.

We climbed over a five barred gate – none of your comfortable stiles or here's-a-gate-that-opens nonsense on the Moors – and set off, walking directly inland, following the East to West route of the Lyke Wake Walk. A Second World War road gave way to a cobbled path as we walked across Jugger Howe Moor, Pepper skipping cheerfully in front of us.

"There are some steps coming up soon, Dad."

"Let's hope they're dry," I muttered.

"What?"

"Nothing."

The steps led down to a beck, and then steeply back up the other side. It was the first time I'd walked down stone steps with Alex. They were old, worn and irregular – but bone dry. Thank you, God. "You go first," I said. "I'll try not to fall too far behind."

The beck at the bottom was beautiful. Roll back the years and it had 'family picnic' written all over it. Or coffee and a bacon sandwich. But we hadn't done a mile yet. And Alex was already marching up the other side...

"Who are all those people?" Alex said half a mile later.

"Looks like a group of walkers coming towards us."

So it was: an orderly, organised, Sunday morning group of walkers. Well wrapped up. Sensible clothes, all wearing jackets and hats despite the sun beating down. The group was led by a man in a green jacket: an official National Park guide I saw as he came closer.

It turned out to be Niedermeyer from *Animal House.* Officious, dictatorial and smug.

"Good morning," I cried, as cheerful as ever.

"Your dog should be on a lead," Niedermeyer said.

"What?"

"Dogs should be on a lead. Nesting birds."

I politely explained that my dog stayed closer to me than Lyra Belacqua's daemon. Bound not by an invisible link but by years of training – and the dog biscuits in my pocket.

"Still should be on a lead," Niedermeyer muttered. "But I'll let it go this time."

Then he stalked off. The group trudged dutifully after him. 'Resigned' was the best way to describe their expressions.

"Shot in the back by his own troops," I said.

"Who?"

"Niedermeyer. *National Lampoon's Animal House.* Honestly, Alex, I feel I've failed you as a father. That's a film you need to watch."

"*Should* the dog be on a lead?" Alex asked before I could bore him senseless with '25 films to watch before you go to university.'

"I don't know. I didn't see a sign. Come to that we haven't seen any birds either."

"Maybe Pepper's frightened them all off..."

I like to think I'm respectful of the countryside. I don't drop litter, I close gates and I carry empty water bottles home with me. But I take the dog. And no, she isn't on a lead. It simply wouldn't have been possible to walk on those paths with a Springer on a lead.

Besides, what was I being asked to do? Protect the local birds so a posse of merchant bankers could blow them out of the sky on August 12th?

I pondered this moral dilemma as we carried on walking uphill. "Is this still the path you were on for D of E?"

"Yeah, it divides just up there. Goes up to the top of the hill."

We discussed his practice expedition with the group from College. Some, it seemed, had not done their training. "They needed a rest every half a mile. Wimps."

I was beginning to know how they felt. I rummaged in my pocket for another slab of Kendal Mint Cake – to which I was becoming increasingly addicted. The Yorkshire walker's epitaph: *Aye, he were a proper walker were your dad. Chemically dependent on Kendal Mint Cake.*

"What's that?" Alex was pointing straight ahead.

"I don't know. It looks like a stone cross."

So it was. Right on top of the Moors, maybe six feet high, standing on a grass plinth and surrounded by a circle of stones. I walked over and read the inscription:

The Lilla Cross. Erected about 620 AD over the reputed grave of Lilla, an officer of the court of Edwin, King of Northumbria, who died saving the life of the King. Believed to be the oldest Christian memorial in the North of England.

"620AD," I said. "1,400 years ago..."

"And probably one of your ancestors, Dad."

"Blimey, you could be right. Wait while I tell Aunty Marjorie..."

Let me explain, just in case there's a family historian reading the book. Aunty Marjorie is my mum's sister. She's long maintained that the family is descended from the ancient kings of Northumberland. Marjorie lives in a semi in Wakefield so it's something of a leap of faith, but here goes...

One such king was named AElla, and mum's maiden name was Ella – which is evidence enough for Aunty Marjorie and me. My wife – having done the genealogical research – says I'm really descended from a wandering Methodist lay preacher on one side and the first editor of the *Guardian* on the other. But I much prefer AElla's story – and on a beautiful Sunday morning with my son at my side, 'Lilla' seemed close enough as well.

"What more could you want?" I said to Alex. "The family's blue blood traced back to the 7th Century. All the lands from Hull to Newcastle rightfully ours..."

One word of warning, gentle reader: if you're squeamish don't go Googling AElla. He met a particularly grisly end at the hands of the Vikings. 'The blood eagle.' Not a good way to go.

"So what's that building?" Alex said as we left our ancestor in peace.

"It's Fylingdales." We'd reached a makeshift road that ran around its perimeter. "It's a radar base. When I was your age it was a Ballistic Missile Early Warning Station. Supposedly gave us four minutes' warning before a Russian bomb arrived. So it's the only thing between us and Vladimir Putin waking up in a bad mood."

"Aren't we a bit close to it?"

"Seeing as we're in touching distance of the fence I think that's a 'yes.'"

Alex looked up the road. "Hang on, Dad, there's a car coming."

Not just a car, a police car. Oh crap. They must have picked us up on CCTV. Or maybe a US spy satellite had spotted us from 200 miles up in space. Thank God Donald Trump would never be in the White House. *Langley, there are two unidentified males approaching the perimeter. Launching drone in three...two...*

I mentally rehearsed our explanation. *Training for a walk, officer. Father and son. Sunday morning. Out with the dog. Sorry, officer, we'll turn around immediately. Ring my wife if you need to. Respected figure in the NHS. She'll vouch for us. Well, one of us...*

It was a police Range Rover. Driving at about ten miles an hour. Two officers in the car. A man and a woman: both young, both with Hollywood mini-series good looks. Chatting and laughing. They waved cheerfully as they passed. I waved back. Clearly terrorists didn't wear faded blue shorts and take a Springer Spaniel with them. Or maybe they had other things on their mind.

"They're driving off towards those woods, Dad."

"Yep. I may be wrong but I'm not entirely sure that catching terrorists is top of their to-do list..."

And lo and behold that narrow escape had taken us up to 4½ miles. Time to eat some more Kendal Mint Cake and retrace our steps.

We walked uneventfully back past Fylingdales, back past Lilla, gazing out across the Moors for eternity, and eventually – after a walk lasting 3 hours, 12 minutes – back to the car.

"So much for Niedermeyer," I said. "We walked nine miles, saw the oldest burial cross in the country and a couple of North Yorkshire's finest off for a quickie in the woods. And not a nesting bird in sight..."

Boots on the Ground

At the start of this book I warned serious walkers to look away. If you *are* a serious walker and you're still with me, then read the next 700 words at your peril. Ring A&E and tell them you'll be along shortly. Mental trauma caused by someone else's stupidity should cover it.

"Cleveland Way, Pennine Way," I'd said to Pepper one bright April morning as the early morning sun glistened off the sea. "How different can they be? Do I really need to spend all that money on walking boots? These walking shoes seem OK..."

At the time 'these walking shoes' *were* OK. Fortunately my first encounter with a flight of stone steps brought me to my senses and boots moved rapidly back up my shopping list. And for Alex as well: yes, he had been "feeling good" when he finished his last D 0f E expedition. But only because he'd walked the last ten miles with his feet inside plastic bags. Not surprisingly, his old boots were now on first name terms with a skip.

As I was rapidly discovering though, walking – at least when you're starting – is not a cheap sport. But for once my brain clicked into gear.

I'd already written a lot about the walk on my blog. I was going to write a lot more and why shouldn't I mention the boots we were wearing?

I pitched the publicity department of two companies. One ignored me, the other – the very wonderful Hi-Tec – marched swiftly to the rescue, and offered to sponsor our boots. "There you are," I said to my wife. "Only been walking for three months and I've turned professional."

And now we were at Go Outdoors in York, having explained to a disappointed young man that he wouldn't be winning 'salesman of the week' but we would like to borrow him while we tried boots on.

Three months ago I was an overweight middle aged bloke that drank too much red wine and ate too much cheese. Now I was going to have walking boots with more go-faster initials than my car.

Hi-Tec had suggested a pair of Altitude PRO RGS: it was love at first sight.

Let's see how they feel...

There's something remarkably stupid about testing a pair of walking boots by strolling around a shop. Carpets have an irritating habit of being level. And three steps up a wooden plank doesn't quite equal climbing remorselessly for two hours. But what else can you do?

Look, mate, I just need to go and walk five miles in these if that's OK. I'll leave my son as security.

I'll ask the manager, sir, but I think it's against company policy to take hostages.

But maybe I don't need to. Because the boots were propelling me forwards. Suddenly I was Jack the Giant Killer devouring the ground in his seven league boots. Two hours remorseless climbing? Bring it on.

"Right, boots sorted," I said to Alex. "We just a need a few other things while we're here..."

I picked up a lifetime's supply of blister plasters and the assorted requirements for battling Mother Nature and her smaller flying creatures.

"Anything else, Dad?" my son asked. "Padded jacket? Rope? Gaiters?"

"What?"

"Gaiters. They go over your ankles and stop everything getting muddy."

"Despite your Mother's comments on my dress sense I'm planning to do this walk in some style. Not look like some geriatric explorer searching for Dr. Livingstone."

"Extra fleece, Dad? Thermal vest?"

"How many times? We're going in the first week of August. We'll be walking through the sun-kissed Yorkshire Dales. The only decision will be factor 8 or factor 10."

"Inflatable canoe?"

Teenage sarcasm, ladies and gentlemen. Once your son has caught this dreadful disease there's no known cure. Then I saw him staring fixedly into a cabinet.

He was looking at a machete. Next to it was a knife that must have been on Freddie Kruger's wish list. So becoming a mass murderer was quite easy. All you had to do was wander in for some mosquito repellent and murmur, "Oh, yes. I almost forgot..."

"I don't think we'll be needing one of those."

"Can't be too careful, Dad. Remember you'll be leaving Yorkshire. Crossing the border into County Durham. The debatable lands..."

"Remind me to speak to your History teacher," I said. "That's the England/Scotland border. Around Carlisle. Now pass me some of that Kendal Mint Cake. It's on special offer..."

Two Weeks to Go

My love affair with the Cleveland Way continued through June and July. But just occasionally I let my devotion slip and strode determinedly up and down the old Scarborough to Whitby railway line.

The great advantage of an old railway line is that it's dead straight and relatively flat: the great disadvantage is that it's dead straight and relatively flat. The walking's easy, but boring. Until yet another middle aged man in Lycra (MAMIL if you want the acronym) comes panting along indulging his Sunday morning Bradley Wiggins fantasy and frightening the dog.

While I was negotiating Team GB and their Olympic daydreams, Alex casually slipped away to the Lake District. Five days and four nights for his gold Duke of Edinburgh expedition – which seemed like an adequate training session...

I'd like to tell you that all this walking in the English summer had made me as brown as the proverbial nut. But where the real Team GB had been warming up for the Rio Olympics in the Pyrenees, I'd been on the Cleveland Way. And it hadn't been a great summer...

All too often I'd watched the mist roll in with the tide: not the most welcome sight when there's eighteen inches between you and the cliff edge.

But with two weeks of my training left, here I was again. Saturday morning, five miles done, five miles from home, all intelligent conversation with the dog exhausted – and back in the fog.

Time to contact my lovely wife. Not that she'd be awake yet but a quick text: a) to wake her up and b) let her know I was still alive.

I don't like stopping when I'm walking. I'm slightly obsessive. It's about keeping the momentum going, not breaking my rhythm.

But clearly I couldn't text while I was walking. Not unless I wanted to be a newspaper headline. *Scarborough man walks over edge of cliff while texting.* At least I'd make it into the Darwin Awards.

So I dictated into my phone. I can't remember the exact words. Something about where I was, how far I'd gone, what time I expected to be home. A simple, loving message that would put a smile on her face when she woke up.

This is what my phone sent:

Good morning. Stop wobbling down about 10 to come home. In the long sleeve top restaurant restaurant for about 10 you slept well

Clearly when my wife received that message there were only three possible explanations: a) I'd given up walking and joined a secret Saturday morning drinking club: b) I'd missed the path in the fog, plunged off the cliff top to the rocks below and – delirious with pain – had tried to send one last, final message to my family: c) the phone reception on a foggy, desolate cliff top wasn't all it might be.

Her reply was short and to the point. *Doesn't make much sense, but assume you're still alive*

Looks like she plumped for option 3, decided not to bother air/sea rescue and went back to sleep...

The Final Countdown

It's 7:45 on Saturday morning. Saturday, July 30th. I've just walked along the cliffs with my faithful training partner. Three miles: just over 53 minutes.

And that's it. Tomorrow, it's Malham. The training is finished, everything we're going to buy has been bought – no, I didn't buy a waterproof coat, there's a limit to how much you can spend – and there'll be just five days and 80 miles to go before Dufton and the welcoming arms of my wife.

It's five months since I asked Alex if he wanted to come with me. Five months since a middle-aged writer decided he needed a physical challenge. Five months since I started walking along the beach at lunchtime. Five months since I weighed far too much and wondered if my left knee would cooperate for five days.

So what's happened since then...

First and foremost I've lost 17.5kg – that's 38lbs in New York and very nearly 3 stone in London. Eat sensibly, fruit for lunch and lots of walking. Those clothes that mocked me when I opened the wardrobe door? They're queuing up to be worn: I've met a lot of old friends.

Since I started wearing my Fitbit on December 26th I've walked a total of 1,094 miles. If you count specific walks – 'boots on' as they say – then I've covered 410 miles. If I'd walked out of my front door and turned left I'd have passed

Aberdeen, passed Inverness and I'd be thinking about lunch in Brora, in the Scottish Highlands. If I'd turned right I'd have reached Arras, in Northern France.

The furthest I've walked is just over 12 miles – north along the Cleveland Way and then back home on the disused Scarborough to Whitby railway line. The shortest day on the Pennine Way is 13¾ miles so, no, I haven't done a dress rehearsal and I most certainly haven't climbed anything remotely resembling the hills I'll face on Monday. Some things have to be taken on trust.

Injuries? None at all. Every sport I've played in my life has seen me visiting A&E: some of them – there's a time to give up squash – have sent me there on a regular basis. Walking has left me fitter, healthier, happier and – miraculously – free of injuries.

But here we are on Saturday morning: this time on Monday the condemned man will be eating a hearty breakfast. I'll be an hour away from Malham Cove, Fountains Fell and Pen y Ghent. It will be time to walk the walk...

The Knight Bus to Malham

Malham is a few miles north of Skipton, in the Yorkshire Dales. If you're driving there, I wouldn't advise anything wider than a bicycle. What you really need is Harry Potter's Knight Bus, a vehicle that will magically shrink itself as yet another 4x4 takes up the whole of the ridiculously narrow country lane. And you'll spend a lot of time in lay-bys pointlessly wondering if the owner of said 4x4 will acknowledge the fact that you've pulled over. But you'll get there in the end. And if it's a Sunday afternoon at the end of July, you'll find that Malham is very, very crowded.

And not just with walkers. With families. 'There are people here with children,' I thought as we drove in. 'That's not right. I'm here to test myself. We're setting off on an epic adventure: the walk of a lifetime. That little girl can't be more than four.'

Maybe I'd been watching too much Bear Grylls. Maybe I'd expected to abseil into Malham from a helicopter. In truth, I wasn't entirely sure *what* I'd expected. As I was to find out in the café, 'Walks around Malham' had been a recent feature on the BBC's *Countryfile*. Result? A village that had exploded.

Beverley – wisely in my view – declined the invitation to stay for tea. "Take care of your dad," she said to Alex. Rather more cryptically she added, "Remember who's in charge." Then she kissed us and climbed back into the car.

"Come on," I said, after we'd unpacked. "Let's go and have a look at Malham Cove. Then we'll have a coffee."

Malham Cove was five minutes' walk up the road from the River House, the first of our five B&Bs. "It looks like something out of *Lord of the Rings*," Alex said as we got our first view of the limestone cliff. He was right. It curved round, almost in a semi-circle. A medieval concert bowl.

"Looks steep," he said.

But I wasn't listening. I was looking at the day trippers. First a small child, now people in flip-flops! There were one or two serious walkers – one with a reassuringly spectacular knee support – but far too many people looked like they were having a pleasant Sunday afternoon stroll. Had they walked to the top of Malham Cove? Surely the Pennine Way wasn't so easy that you could tackle it in flip-flops? Had I wasted my time with all that training?

I wasn't exactly looking to see a 'fatalities this year' sign by the side of the path. I did want to see some people in pain.

Dave Parker's Rabbit Pie

Time to eat. The bridge over the beck was strictly one person at a time. We tiptoed across and found the Secret Cove bistro. "This looks good," I said. "Slightly more upmarket than the pub."

"Sorry," said Mrs Secret Cove, "Fully booked."

"We're embarking on an epic adventure," I said.

"Fully booked," she said.

And so we retreated to the pub across the road. The Buck: the dark, brooding Buck. It wasn't hard to imagine Voldemort and Lucius Malfoy closeted in a corner. Bev and I had eaten at the pub in Middleham. This was the same: it was a pub for locals in a village increasingly dependent on tourism. We weren't made to feel unwelcome – but 'tolerated' is probably the word I'm looking for.

"Award winning Malhamdale sausages," Alex said, reading through the menu at hungry teenage boy speed.

I saw his award winning sausages and raised him a rabbit pie. "Locally shot by Dave Parker," I said. "Not many snipers get a mention on the menu."

Snipers but not, apparently, fishermen. There was trout, caught by 'the landlord and his mate.' "Maybe they weren't supposed to catch the trout," Alex said. "Maybe the landlord's mate is the local policeman."

Speaking as someone who's conspicuously failed to catch a fish in his entire adult life I'd have demanded a name check and taken my chances.

Alex decided his first meal on the Pennine Way would be courtesy of Dave Parker. With some scepticism, I went for the award-winning sausages. "That's the problem isn't it?" the grumpy old man inside me said. "Everything's 'award-winning' these days. Or 'world famous.' There are at least three chip shops on Scarborough sea front advertising 'our world famous fish and chips.' I suspect they talk of little else in Los Angeles."

Enough cynicism, here was Tracey with the grub. Blimey, the spirit of my dad was alive and well and working in the Buck's kitchen. The cabbage looked like it had been boiled for days.

She was back five minutes later with the obligatory "Is everything alright for you?"

We answered with the equally obligatory "Lovely, thanks" despite the near certainty that the judging for the 'Award winning sausages' had been done by the butcher's wife.

"So this is the rabbit that was shot by Dave Parker?" I said, indicating Alex's pie.

"Yeah," Tracey replied. "Dave is my dad's best mate." Memo to the young bucks of Malham. Not a girl to be courted lightly.

"Is he a good shot then?"

"Awesome. He shoots 'em through the head so there's no shot in them."

As my son had just finished Dave's rabbit pie I filed that under 'good news.' And as no-one had shot, caught or snared the banoffee pie we passed on dessert.

The Hearty Breakfast

The deal was simple. I would wake Alex at 7:30. That would give us plenty of time for breakfast and we'd start walking at 9:00.

So inevitably I woke up at 5:30. Normally, that's not a problem. I am by nature one of God's early risers – and I like it that way. I go downstairs, feed the animals, drink a glass of 50/50 orange and grapefruit juice, read the news, check my e-mails and occasionally pick up my (very light) weights and pretend I'm working out. And I enjoy the time to myself.

But when you're trapped in a strange bedroom it's a different story. What the hell was I going to *do* for the next two hours?

I dutifully tapped *Riverhouse1* into my iPad and read the news. *All* the news. I wrote my notes on Malhamdale's award winning sausages and sent a text to Beverley. I read every word that had ever been written on the Malham to Horton-in-Ribblesdale section of the Pennine Way. Twice.

And I worried about whether I'd make it through the day.

Furthest distance covered in training, 12 miles. Along what I was beginning to suspect was a very easy stretch of the Cleveland Way and a very flat railway line. Had I been training for the Tour de France by cycling to the corner shop?

But we were here. And I was pleased. Pleased the waiting was over. Pleased the challenge had finally arrived. Above all, pleased I was facing it with my son.

I crept out of bed and turned the shower on. Not the best start to the day. My daughter had cried on me with more force. But I had no aches and pains. I'd come through the training. Now all I had to do was walk for five days...

I got dressed. Lucky pants, shorts, t-shirt. And Ray Mears. Technically 'Ray' was a gilet from Mountain Warehouse. Slightly overpriced at £19.99 but it had more pockets than you could count. Phone, Kendal Mint Cake, tissues, notebook, pen, 500ml bottle of water – they all disappeared without trace and I'd barely scratched the surface. "Ray Mears has got a jacket like that, Dad," Alex said when I first put it on. And as I think 'gilet' is about the most pretentious word in the English language, it's been 'Ray Mears' ever since.

I woke Alex. "Let's go," I said. "Cometh the hour, cometh the father and son."

But not before breakfast. The River House dining room was like the Buck: dark and uninspiring. And empty. "Maybe everyone else is starting later than us, Dad..."

'Everyone' was a relative term. How could there be so many 'vacancies' signs on August 1st? Five weeks earlier the UK had voted 'Leave:' the pound had plunged. The entire nation was supposed to be on staycation while tumbleweed blew along the Spanish beaches.

Whether she'd voted 'Remain' or there was some other reason, Mrs Riverhouse didn't look happy. I occasionally have a fantasy about running a B&B in an isolated beauty spot. But I suspect the reality is rather different. The constant battles with guests, suppliers and Trip Advisor must take their toll. And then along comes Airbnb to turn us all into guest houses. I made a mental note to tap 'divorce statistics for B&Bs' into Google...

Two middle-aged French women arrived. We dutifully said 'good morning' and they dutifully ordered a full English: then they stared at it with that special expression – a mixture of awe and disgust – that the French save for a full English breakfast. But credit where le crédit is due: they ploughed through it.

If I have an occasional fantasy about running a B&B I have a permanent fantasy about breakfast in France. Sitting outside, coffee, croissants, French bread... Is the opposite true? Is there someone in Poitou-Charente waking up every morning with a secret longing for black pudding, award-winning sausages and a fried egg?

"What would you like in your sandwiches?" Breakfast was over. Now we were with Mr Riverhouse, negotiating the terms of our packed lunch.

"What are our choices?"

"Cheese or ham."

Blimey. Cutting edge. I asked for one of each. At least Alex could take his pick.

"Pickle on your cheese? Dab of mustard on the ham?"

"Just a smear of mustard," I said, remembering my James Herriot. A 'dab' in the Dales would be uneatable to a wimp like me.

"How far are you going?" he asked.

"Dufton," I said. "Five days. The wife's picking us up on Friday afternoon. Well," I added, "Unless she's changed her mind after a week without me."

He laughed and handed me the packed lunches. We went back upstairs and Alex put them in the backpack. Our enormous orange backpack.

Another confession. I was feeling guilty about the backpack. I'd made a list of what we needed to take with us every day: then Alex had taken over and made a proper list. Now it was all in the backpack. While he was in the shower I'd casually lifted it up. I suspect the SAS invade countries with less weight on their backs.

"Are you sure?" I said again. "We can do morning and afternoon. Or an hour each."

"No," he said. "I'll do today. You carry it tomorrow."

Both Bev and I had suggested two smaller backpacks. But there was the 40 litre waterproof monster from college lying in our hall, still not returned from his D of E expedition – and with all the straps, supports and waterproof covers you could ever need. "No point wasting the money," Alex had said. So we didn't.

And now we were standing outside the River House B&B in Malham. It was time to go.

But I couldn't just start walking. "Wait a minute," I said. "I want to say something."

"What?"

I wanted to tell Alex that the day he shrugged and said, "Sure, I like walking with you" he changed my life. I wanted to say that he'd given me the chance to do something that I'd thought was impossible. That if he hadn't said 'yes' I'd still be three stone overweight with a wardrobe of clothes I couldn't wear.

I wanted to say that whatever happened over the next five days, nothing would beat that simple moment of setting off – of keeping a commitment we'd made to each other. I wanted to say that every minute of the training was worth it just to be standing outside the River House B&B with my son.

I wanted to say that just by coming with me he'd given me the most precious gift he could ever give me.

I wanted to say...

But 17 year old boys are not big on emotional speeches. Especially from their dad. So I said, "Thanks." And added, "Thanks for coming with me. Thanks for giving me the chance to do this. I'm really grateful. And I love you."

"You're welcome," my son said. And he started walking up the hill towards Malham Cove – and five days with his dad.

Part 2: The Walk
At Last...

It was August 1st: Yorkshire Day. How appropriate.

Out of Malham, and gently uphill. The sun was shining, I was wearing shorts. How easy was this? And there was the medieval amphitheatre in front of us. 'Pennine Way' the sign said. That would be us, then.

We walked across a pleasantly even path – looking reassuringly like the inviting Google images I'd seen – and past three sun-bathing cows. Not exactly the cheering crowds of *le Grand Depart*, but they'd have to do.

"If it's all like this it's going to be easy," the team optimist said.

The team realist sighed. He may have muttered "amateur" under his breath. I didn't quite catch it.

And less than a mile after leaving the B&B we came to the first climb of the day. 400 steps up Malham Cove: 400 uneven steps, 260 feet up.

But just like the steps on the Cleveland Way I told myself. 'You'll need a rest,' the guide books had said. 'Take the chance to pause and look back.' No thanks, climbing steps is about momentum for me: keeping going. Besides, I couldn't let the orange pack get too far in front of me.

"Are you alright, Dad?"

"Yeah, I'm good." *Was that gentle encouragement? Or was he worried about me already?*

We were at the top. And I did pause and look back. Not so much at the view, but at the path, winding back towards Malham. To acknowledge that we'd left base camp behind. That five days of walking with my son had moved from theory to reality. That 'Father, Son and the Pennine Way' had finally started.

"The limestone pavement, Dad. We're supposed to be wowed."

"The guide book says 'You can't resist leaping about on them.'"

"Think it through, Dad."

Alex was right. With five days to go, 'leaping about' within the first 15 minutes seemed a tad frivolous. Besides, there was my long history of falling over. I could hear the phone call...

Yeah, sorry, Mum. Could you come and fetch me? Dad's fallen over ... his ankle I think ... leaping around on a limestone pavement at the top of Malham Cove ... of course I told him not to ... but you know what he's like ... yeah, he's being winched into a helicopter now ... yes, of course I'll video it for you ... how far had we got? About half a mile...

"This was in the Harry Potter film wasn't it?" Alex said.

"Which one?"

"*Deathly Hallows.* The scene where Harry and Hermione have that dance."

And that was it. We were off. We turned our back on the limestone pavement, found the next signpost and started walking. And it was like it always was. The two of us, walking and talking. Just without the dog, and with five days of conversation ahead of us. Obviously we started with one of life's great mysteries...

"I still can't understand it," I said.

"What?"

"Harry Potter. Why he preferred Ginny Weasley to Hermione."

But Alex had a more serious point to make. "I kind of grew up with Harry Potter didn't I?"

"You kind of grew up watching your brother and sister watching Harry Potter. I think you were exposed to the darker films at an earlier age than they were. Maybe that's why we've been able to discuss deeper subjects with you. Exposed to Voldemort while you were still in nursery."

"I might need counselling..."

I didn't think so. A holiday on the Norfolk coast: we'd seen the latest Harry Potter at a cinema in Norwich. *Order of the Phoenix*? The one where Sirius Black died. Alex would have been seven or eight. I'd driven back to the holiday cottage discussing good and evil with him.

I reached for my iPhone as we walked through a valley. Started to take photos that I knew would disappoint me. Good photographs take time to compose. If I'd learned one thing from having an office next to a photographer it was that.

And there was that other valuable lesson I'd learned on the Cleveland Way. Concentrate on the path, not on the photograph.

His ankle I think ... no, he survived the limestone pavement ... fell over taking a photograph ... no, no, we managed a mile ... helicopter? No, we were right at the bottom of a steep valley ... they strapped him onto a mule.

We came to Malham Tarn. So far so good. Alex was re-fuelling with Haribos and I was continuing my love affair with Kendal Mint Cake. And feeling ambitious...

"I'd like to do this every year," I said. "You know, just the two of us, as long as I'm physically capable."

"OK. That's cool. Where next?"

"I don't know. Somewhere warm. We probably ought to fly. I'm feeling guilty about asking your Mum to drive to Malham and then asking her to take a day off to pick us up."

"Why don't we walk across Japan?"

What? Where did that come from? And how wide was Japan anyway?

"We wouldn't be able to read the signs. What's 'Pennine Way' in Japanese? What about the West Highland Way?"

"I thought you said somewhere warm?"

"Southern Ireland?"

"That's not warm either."

It didn't matter did it? So long as it was the two of us. But even as we talked about possibilities I knew the odds were against me. Next year Alex had his A-levels. Then he was off to university. Sooner or later there'd be the First Serious Girlfriend. His dad and his walking boots would slip down the priority list. One of the reasons these five days were so important to me.

"What's that?"

"It's Malham Water House, where Charles Kingsley was inspired to write *The Water Babies*. Now it's a Field Studies Centre."

"So why are all those people staring into the grass?"

"Because they're students and that's what students do."

We walked around the back of what had once been Lord Ribblesdale's modest little shooting box and past a ridiculously large sculpture of a spider. And then we were down the lane and turning right into a field, the hills rising on both sides of us.

"Do you think I should have bought a waterproof jacket?" I said.

"Too late now..."

"That's true. There was a guy wearing a really nice one on *Countryfile* last week. I found it online and e-mailed myself the link."

"It wasn't red was it?" Alex said. "Don't ever buy a red jacket. All the assessors on D of E wear red jackets. They're completely up themselves. They all think they're a combination of Bear Grylls and Hawkeye. Whatever you do, Dad, don't ever get a red jacket. Anyway, what colour was it?"

"Blue," I lied.

We turned a corner and saw an old man, about 200 yards ahead of us.

Well, we'd soon overhaul him.

Ten minutes later, we hadn't. So much for bounding up Malham Cove. Had all my training been a waste of time? And what did it say about my chances of lasting out five days if I couldn't catch a pensioner after five miles?

But on the other hand I could see my future self. Striding across the fells, younger walkers left toiling in my wake, burnt nut brown by a life in the sun. Living to 108 on a diet of seeds and berries...

"What time do you want lunch, Dad?"

...Or ham sandwiches and salt and vinegar crisps.

"Not yet. I've seen the sandwiches remember. When we're at the top of a hill. I want to eat lunch with the Dales spread out beneath me."

The thought of salt n' vinegar crisps must have released some adrenalin. Suddenly we'd caught the old man.

Well-worn boots and a weather-beaten backpack. No concession to age or walking poles.

He had a retired schoolmaster's face. Or maybe he'd worked for the local council. A well-earned retirement after 40 years of rejecting over-ambitious planning applications in the National Park. No, a schoolmaster. Chemistry, and afternoons on the rugby pitch.

"Good morning," I said. "Grand day."

"Not bad." A suitably understated response for the Yorkshire Dales.

"Going far?"

"Ten miles. Round trip. Back in time for lunch."

"Well, enjoy your day..."

"Do you think you'll do that when you're retired, Dad?" Alex asked after we'd put a respectable distance between us.

"I hope so. Besides, it'd give your Mum some peace. She hasn't watched the box set of *Breaking Bad* yet. And it's probably the secret of a happy marriage. Disappear for ten miles every morning."

We walked through a gap in a dry stone wall and the path divided. Left and up the hill: straight on along the bottom of the valley. I fished the map out of my pocket and started to wrestle with it, my inexperience all too apparent. Mark Richards' Law of Map-reading: wherever I wanted to be on the map needed the maximum number of folds to get there.

"Pennine Way?" Our chemistry teacher had caught us up. "Straight up." And with that he headed along the bottom of the valley, towards an appointment with his wife and his lunch.

'Straight up' was fine as directions go. There was unquestionably a hill: there was a farm 400 yards to our right. What there wasn't was a path.

"Is that a sign on the fence up there, Dad?"

"Do you want me to go and check?" Thanks, pal. 'Up there' was 300 yards straight uphill through thick grass. So much for paving stones and well-defined paths.

"There must be a path somewhere. Can you see if the grass has been trodden down?"

Meanwhile Mr Bunsen-Burner disappeared round a bend, no doubt chuckling smugly to himself at our incompetence and having an erotic fantasy about his wife's tomato chutney.

I'd just resigned myself to plodding uphill to check the sign when help appeared in the shape of a remarkably fit looking Scandinavian. He arrived in a blur of electric blue.

"You are walking the Pennine Way?"

"We are..."

"Is a challenge, yes?"

And he was gone. But so were our navigation problems. "Follow him," we said in unison. We marched up Fountains Fell, following the electric blue beacon. The gap was steadily increasing but on a day like today he'd be visible from Stockholm. And then, nearly at the top of the hill, we saw him stop. "Ha!" I said, "He's exhausted. We've beaten him."

No, he was just having his lunch. Sitting on a rock, gazing down into the valley and — "What's that, Dad? It smells like that café you took us into in Amsterdam" — smoking a reflective joint.

We carried on climbing and the sun continued to shine. "The map says we're in an area of shake holes." I felt compelled to share the occasional geographical tidbit with my son.

"What's a shake hole then?"

"Er... I think it's when the ground has sunk."

"You should have paid more attention at school, Dad."

Alex could talk. Once he'd seen a satnav at work he'd effectively resigned from Geography lessons.

Ten minutes more climbing and we were at the top. And face to face with our first cairn. 48 hours later I'd be staggering, soaked to the skin, from one pile of stones to the next. For now I dutifully joined the ranks of walkers who'd put their stone on the top and posed for a picture. The view was spectacular — but at 2,192 feet, so was the wind. "Why don't we go down there in that hollow, Dad?"

I might have stayed with the view. But Alex was right. We scrambled down into the hollow and found a couple of flat rocks to sit on. The first morning done. According to the app on my phone we'd done 8.35 miles. So about six, maybe 6½ to go.

I was feeling good. More than good. We'd done eight miles. Two fairly strenuous climbs. We hadn't got lost, we hadn't fallen out. We'd talked all the way, met a couple of people – and I was fine. I was keeping up with Alex. True, he was carrying the pack. I looked back down Fountain's Fell and muttered a prayer. Just let it be flat tomorrow. No hills, please, Lord...

We sat on the rocks and traded packets of crisps. Another of Alex's many qualities: every family needs a child that likes salt n' vinegar crisps. Mercifully he'd inherited the gene from somewhere.

"Are you ready to set off, Dad?" he said twenty minutes later.

"Sure," I said. "I just need a pee first." I wandered twenty yards, checked there was no-one coming up the hill and – I had at least learned something on the cliff top – made sure the wind was behind me. And while I stood there, admiring the view and peeing cheerfully on a clump of heather the season changed. Summer had surrendered to autumn. I turned around and the temperature had dropped ten degrees. The sun had gone, the wind had strengthened – it couldn't really be this strong in August could it? – and as Pen y Ghent came into view an ominous black cloud hung over the top of it.

"Dear God," I said. "Have we got to go all the way down into the valley and then back up over Pen y Ghent?"

"I don't think the National Parks people would approve a bridge..."

"You're probably right. Hey, look," I said, brightening up, "There's a shaft of sunlight glinting off some cars down there. That must be the car park at the bottom of Pen y Ghent. There's bound to be an ice cream van. Come on, I'll buy you one..."

Pen y Ghent

There wasn't an ice-cream van: just three parked cars. A couple were sitting on the tailgate of one of them having a genteel, civilised picnic. They even had a bottle of wine. It had taken us the best part of an hour to come down from the top of Fountains Fell and trudge along the road. I was tired, I was hungry and I'd fantasised about food all the way. "What do you think? Should we mug them?"

"Too many witnesses, Dad."

I glanced up at the top of Pen y Ghent one more time. Was that really the path? It couldn't be. It was vertical. I shook my head, pushed the gate open and started walking uphill. Again...

We passed a solitary group of walkers coming down. 'Pen y Ghent can be very crowded,' the guide book had said. Not today. The beginning of August, the school holidays, a sunny day – and three cars in the car park. No wonder there hadn't been an ice cream van.

"That can't be the path," I said.

"I think it is."

"But it goes straight up the side of the mountain."

"Technically it's a hill, Dad."

"So when does a hill become a mountain?"

My son sighed. "Don't stop to Google it, Dad. Just keep walking. It's the only way we're going to reach the B&B."

In truth I was trying to distract myself. Whether Pen y Ghent was a hill or a mountain the path *did* go straight up the side. Fountains Fell had been a long walk up a hill. This was going to be a climb.

I looked up again. My fear of heights stirred: the Dementors liked what they saw. I could feel them flexing their muscles. But Alex was right. There *was* only one way to reach the B&B, and that way was straight up.

And then we met two children. A tousle-haired brother and sister. Maybe eight and nine. Skipping merrily down the path, arguing about who was the best. Followed by two very fit parents: a mother who clearly had 'triathlon' crossed off her list well before breakfast.

"Hi," I said, smiling my I'm-also-a-remarkably-fit-parent smile, "Have the children been to the top?"

"Of course," in a what-else-would-they-do tone of voice. And with that they were gone, presumably to kayak down the Swale before bedtime.

I relaxed slightly. It wouldn't pass the head teacher's risk assessment, but if two children could climb Pen y Ghent how difficult could it be?

Suddenly it *was* crowded. We overtook a group of three old people (sadly making them not much older than me) and now there were three 'lads' behind us. Talking in banter as lads are legally obliged to do. They were from Sheffield. News of a night out floated up the hill. One of them – Wayne probably: his mother was unlikely to have christened him Waz – had a laugh so irritating that any sane person would have had it surgically removed.

Now the serious climb had started. And Alex's adrenalin had kicked in. Whether he meant to or not he was going faster. I was trying to keep up with him. Didn't want him to think he had to slow down. And I had to keep ahead of the lads: go faster than I wanted to. Don't look down, I told myself, don't look down...

I scrambled faster. Started listing to my left to keep my centre of gravity into the hill. Now the Dementors scented blood. 'It's the only way we're going to reach the B&B, Dad.' Alex was right: I tried to speed up, scrambling over the rocks. Looked down. Mistake.

'Did you see that, Waz?' 'What, Gaz?' 'Grey haired bloke looked down. Slipped and went over the edge.' 'Nurrh, nurrh, nurrh. Top bantz, mate.'

Christ, this was hard. I'd trained for this by walking up the steps between the beach chalets. Then I'd progressed to steps on the Cleveland Way. What was it the army said about proper preparation?

"You alright, Dad?"

"Yeah, yeah," I lied. "I'm good." I was really scrambling now, not ashamed of using my hands to steady me. "Is it much further?"

"Don't think so..."

Another silent prayer, this time of thanks.

It wasn't much further. One more scramble. One last hand-up from my son and I was walking on paving stones. And a minute later, finally at the summit.

There were half a dozen people there. I overheard one man telling his girlfriend that on a clear day you could see the Irish Sea. "But today's too cloudy." Really? We were so high up I had a decent view of New York.

"Stand there," I said to Alex. "I need a photo of you." And as I took the photo I realised he'd carried the pack up Pen y Ghent. I'd been so obsessed with myself I'd simply followed the orange pack up 2,277 feet. The orange pack I'd struggled to lift...

We had a drink of water and started down the other side. With the cloud swirling in there was no other choice. "How far do you think it is?" Alex said.

"I don't know. Two miles maybe? I'm beginning to think that all the websites were a bit out with their estimates. That's Horton down there isn't it?"

It was. A tiny speck in the distance. But it was all downhill and we'd get there eventually. And it had a pub, a bed and – God willing – a power shower.

The World's Worst Curry

It took us an hour to reach Horton. I was rapidly learning a basic Pennine Way rule. Just because you can see something – or somewhere – it doesn't mean you're nearly there.

"Where are we staying?"

"The Willows. Hawes Road. It's round a bend." I was too tired to look at the map. But there was a girl approaching.

"Here we go. Throw the SatNav away. I'll wind the window down and ask."

The girl was Polish. Goodness knows what she was doing in Horton-in-Ribblesdale and she hadn't yet mastered its geography. Her directions would have seen us walk straight into the River Ribble. But she had a lovely smile.

The Willows was for sale. We were welcomed by Mr Willows. I got the distinct impression that Mrs Willows hadn't been seen for some time. One more tick in the 'Running a B&B may be bad for your marriage' column.

And a tick for 'your bags have arrived' as well. When I hadn't been worrying about keeping up with Alex or falling off Pen y Ghent I'd had a few nagging doubts about the bags. Would someone really take them from one B&B to the next? Yes: there they were, nestled snugly in the hall.

"Good day?" Mr Willows asked.

"Tiring," I said. "But yeah. Very good."

"Are you doing all the Pennine Way?"

"Some of it," I said. "We finish on Friday. My wife's picking us up in Dufton. Unless she's changed her mind after a week without me."

Alex must have been tired. He stifled a yawn at the side of me.

We walked through the kitchen and to our room. But not before I looked out of the kitchen window. What a view. Or, as the BBC would now insist on writing it, What. A. View.

Pen y Ghent in all its glory. Wow. What a wonderful kitchen to cook in. I could just see myself standing there, preparing the Spag Bol. Gazing at the summit as it drifted in and out of the clouds. Paying no attention to the knife as it drifted off the onion and into my finger...

The room was lovely. "Coffee?" I asked Alex. But he had more pressing concerns. He'd been walking through the dark ages for eight hours.

"What's the Wi-Fi password?"

"I'm too tired to look for it," I said. "It'll be Willows1."

A fairly safe guess. B&B passwords are not complicated. If you're staying at River House it's Riverhouse1 – or something very close to it. If you've got all your fingers you'll get there...

"No, it isn't."

"Alright, Willows99."

He dutifully tapped it into his phone. "It's not that either."

"Upper case W?"

"Nope."

Damn it, I had to look it up. And this one was complicated. So complicated that Mr Willows clearly thought Vladimir Putin would soon get bored with choosing the next US President and turn his attention to Yorkshire B&Bs instead.

An hour later we were showered, restored – or at least as restored as a sachet of Nescafe and two Bourbon Creams can make you – and we'd not disturbed the Kremlin. It was time for dinner.

Mr Willows recommended the Crown on the grounds that it was the only pub in the village. I looked at the map. "It says 'New Inn' on the map?"

"That's the bridge," he said.

"So the pub's called the Crown and the bridge is called the New Inn?"

"Yep."

Clearly Horton had its own naming system. *Pound of mince and some sausages? You'll be wanting the Black Bull.* No wonder our Polish girl hadn't learned her way around the village.

"Will you be able to do us a packed lunch in the morning?" I asked Mr Willows as we left.

Our host stared at us wild-eyed. "You didn't order it in advance." Cripes. Were we supposed to? Why didn't you drop me an e-mail two days before we arrived? "There isn't a shop in the village," he offered as an excuse.

And there's me thinking running a B&B might involve keeping some food in. "I might have a bit of tuna downstairs," he muttered. Let's hope he's not snowed in for the winter. *B&B owner survives two months on can of tuna and own foot.*

"Can we get anything on the way?"

"What? There's nothing between here and Hawes."

He said it with such a terrified expression that I immediately thought I was in a 1930s Sherlock Holmes film. *What? You can't go out there, Mr Richards. There's nothing between here and Hawes but the grimp and the mire.*

"I'll ask at the pub," I said. "Don't worry about it."

Sadly I did ask – and did order – two packed lunches from the Crown. Memo to self: eat their food first, order their packed lunch second.

The food was spectacular. It will live long in my memory. As will the smell of the cyclist standing next to me at the bar. Blue and yellow Lycra, legs knotted with muscles, not an ounce of fat – and a very strong smell of vinegar.

Is that what happens to you after ten hours in the saddle? Your sweat turns to vinegar? Or do cyclists furtively douse themselves in Sarson's Malt to keep the flies away? The cool down area after a stage of the Tour de France must be a remarkable experience.

I tried not to breathe in and ordered a beef curry. "Alex, have you decided?"

"I'm tired, Dad, I only want soup." What? A teenage boy so tired he only wanted soup? At the time I was surprised. At the time I hadn't carried the backpack...

Let me repeat: the food at the Crown was spectacular. It was by some distance the worst curry I have ever eaten. Maybe the pub should have had an alias after all. *Bad review on TripAdvisor? Not us, mate, that'll be the New Inn. Or the Black Bull...*

The curry was self-evidently Sunday's home-made steak pie filling performing an encore. For the first time in my life I had to add English mustard to a curry to heat it up. Pepper would have eaten it – but she'd only have described it as 'adequate.'

But at least they had the good manners not to describe it as 'Ribblesdale Award Winning Curry...'

When does a Hill become a Mountain?

Monday night. Alex was sleeping soundly. But I was wide awake, the adrenalin still rushing round my body.

I was still climbing Pen y Ghent. I could still feel the rocks beneath my feet. Still see the path in front of me, hear the people below me. Still see the view – and the drop at the side of me.

I'd gone further outside my comfort zone than I could ever have imagined.

What a hill that was.

Then a thought struck me as I lay in bed listening to my son's breathing. Had Alex been right? 'Technically it's a hill, Dad.' Or was Pen y Ghent a mountain?

Don't be stupid, I told myself. It's a hill. You're a writer, remember? 'Hunched over a keyboard all day.' You don't climb mountains.

I'd wanted a physical challenge. Wanted to spend time with my son. I'd asked him to come for a walk with me. The word 'mountain' had never even crossed my mind.

But suddenly there was pride at stake. If I *had* climbed a mountain there were bragging rights. The chance to bore my wife senseless for years to come.

Five days later I was back in front of my laptop and I asked Google. *When does a hill become a mountain?* Clearly I wasn't the only one wondering: there were 10.7m results. And yes! The headline answer was the one I wanted.

Unlike many other landforms, there is no universally accepted definition of a mountain. Many geographers state that a mountain is 300 metres (1,000 feet) above sea level. Other definitions, such as the one in the Oxford English Dictionary, put the hill limit at twice that.

1,000 feet was ridiculous. The cliffs on the Cleveland Way were 500 feet and I walked up those with the dog. But no-one should disagree with the OED. According to their definition, at 2,277 feet Pen y Ghent was comfortably a mountain.

But even as I read the definition, I still wasn't convinced. Surely a mountain demands more than just a measurement? Snow, crampons, someone looking dramatically into the camera and talking about a 'window in the weather?'

And sure enough, Google's next entry was a lot less supportive:

There is no universally accepted definition of a mountain. Elevation, volume, relief, steepness, spacing and continuity have all been used as criteria for defining a mountain. In the OED a mountain is defined as "a natural elevation of the earth surface rising more or less abruptly from the surrounding level and attaining an altitude which, relative to the adjacent elevation, is impressive or notable."

Well Pen y Ghent ticked the last three boxes. And it was higher than Cuilcagh in Ireland and Snaefell in the Isle of Man, both listed by themountainguide.co.uk

But try as I might I couldn't persuade myself that I'd climbed a mountain. Snowdon and Ben Nevis were mountains. Pen y Ghent wasn't. Much as I'd like it to be.

I tentatively discussed it with my wife. Maybe my timing wasn't spot on: we'd just watched *Everest*.

She snorted scornfully. "Don't be ridiculous. Pen y Ghent's a hill. People climb it on Geography field trips. You climbed a hill, sweetheart. And besides," she added, playing her trump card. "If you have to ask whether it's a mountain, it isn't."

"But…"

"But nothing. It's like childbirth. If you have to ask if your wife is in labour she isn't."

I sighed. She was right. And those two children we'd passed had climbed it. And children *definitely* don't climb mountains. Well, not unless they're with Julie Andrews…

And then something wonderful happened. Any man who's been married for 20 years will tell you there's no better feeling than your wife eating a large slice of humble pie. Beverley stumbled across a story on the BBC website:

Calf Top Hill re-categorised as a Mountain

New state-of-the-art measuring technology used by the Ordnance Survey has calculated that Calf Top in the Yorkshire Dales stands at 609.602 metres high.

The recognised threshold for when a hill becomes a mountain is 609.6m (2,000 feet) so Calf Top is 2mm above the required height.

Two millimetres? But you have to draw a line somewhere. And if a pimple like Calf Top was a mountain, Pen y Ghent was *definitely* a mountain. And that night a middle-aged mountaineer fell asleep with a broad smile on his face...

Tuesday: "I think we should have turned right..."

"You OK with the internet for ten minutes?" I said to Alex. "Breakfast is at eight. I'm just going down to the pub for the packed lunches."

"Why don't we get them on the way?"

"Because 'the way' is the other way. We turn left out of the front door."

"Are you sure?"

"I was looking at the map while you were in the shower."

He shrugged and went back to WhatsApp'ing with Vladimir Putin. I walked down to the pub, trying not to think about my date with the backpack.

The first person I saw was Vinegar Joe, hunched over a bowl of Rice Krispies. And still wearing yesterday's Lycra: going the long way round the dining room seemed sensible. I pushed the kitchen door open. "Come to collect two packed lunches."

"What name?"

"Richards." Spelled F-O-O-L.

Fifteen quid for two packed lunches. It made six strawberries at Wimbledon look cheap. Then again there was 'nothing between here and Hawes, Mr Richards.' Who cares about value for money when you control the local monopoly?

I walked back through the dining room, asked Joe if he was going far – he was, but mercifully in the opposite direction – and strolled back to the B&B, thinking about my breakfast and Ikea instructions.

I've been outwitted by them for the whole of my adult life. Actually, I've been outwitted by *everyone's* instructions. I've been totally unable to relate the dowel, the locking nut – the whatever-it-is-I'm-holding-in-my-hand – to the diagram on the floor.

I've also gone through my adult life totally unable to recognise people. If I see someone – even someone I know well – where I'm not expecting to see them, I don't recognise them. Cue enormous embarrassment and a stilted conversation as I search desperately for clues.

"So, er... what are you doing now?"

"I'm still married to you, Mark."

Ha, ha – I'm joking – but only just.

Instructions. Can't recognise anyone. I put two and two together and assumed it was just me: that I had some rare form of face/diagram dyslexia that medical science hadn't yet discovered. Then about five years ago I stumbled across an article on prosopagnosia – face blindness – and found that 1-2% of the population have the same problem.

That made me feel a lot better. Now I warn anyone I meet that next time I see them I won't recognise them. But given that I can't understand a basic diagram and can barely recognise my wife you may wonder why I'd decided I'd be fine with an Ordnance Survey map.

Because I'm a man. Because I'd felt embarrassed on Monday. Alex had carried the pack and – in the moments when we weren't following our electric blue Scandinavian – he'd navigated.

Today, it was my turn. And damn it I was his dad, the alpha male, the expedition leader. Richards of the Dales.

So, yes – while Alex had been in the shower I'd been poring over the map. The road went round to the left. That's where the B&B was. And it was on Hawes Road. And Hawes was north of us. Or left as I looked at the map.

"Out of the door and turn left," I said over a remarkably fine full English.

"Are you sure?" Alex asked again.

"Stop worrying. Take it easy today. I'll carry the pack and I'll navigate. Have a day off."

My son looked doubtful. Mr Willows paused, glanced sceptically at me, then went back to making the coffee.

Half an hour later we fastened our boots and stepped outside. "You ready, Dad?"

"No problem at all."

Alex lifted the pack onto my shoulder. "Oooofff," I said and staggered forwards.

"You won't notice it after five minutes." Somehow I doubted that, but man points were at stake. I couldn't show weakness in front of my son.

"Turn left remember," I grunted.

"We should have seen a sign by now," I said after I'd managed five hundred painful yards.

It was the first time in my life I'd carried a pack: something else I should have practised. Or maybe I was planning to take my son along as a Sherpa for the rest of my life...

The pack had changed my centre of gravity. I was bent forward, every movement I made was exaggerated. Meanwhile the village had ended. Hawes Road dutifully bent round to the left. In front of us a track disappeared into a copse of trees.

"Is that it?"

"Surely it would have a sign?" I said.

The track went into the trees for twenty yards and then petered out. It looked a damn fine place to park the car if you were 18 and with your girlfriend. But it wasn't the Pennine Way. I walked round the bend: 20 yards up the road there was a railway bridge. A railway bridge that – according to my reading of the map – some fool had built in completely the wrong place.

As gently as he could, Alex reached across and took the map from me. "I think we should have turned right, Dad."

We plodded back to the B&B. Did the curtains twitch sarcastically as we finally set off in the right direction? 15 minutes wasted: 15 extra minutes carrying the pack. But at least Henry the Navigator was leading the way, not Blind Jack of Knaresborough.

Reflections on Horton

Alex is clearly destined for a career in the diplomatic service. He didn't say 'told you so' as we passed the pub. Twenty more yards and we turned left to begin a long, slow climb up a farm track covered in loose stones.

"So what did you make of Horton?" I said. I needed a conversation or I'd start thinking about the weight of the pack.

Alex shrugged. "Alright, I suppose. Just a village."

"But a village with Pen y Ghent in its back garden. Yet it was deserted on August 1st."

"So what are you saying?"

"I'm saying that Horton is a village that's in the right place at the right time. That's had a fantastic business opportunity presented to it by an accident of geography. But did we feel welcome? The pub served the world's worst curry, ripped us off over the packed lunches and boasted about having no internet. The only person who smiled at us was the Polish girl."

"Are you going to write that in the book?"

"There's no point writing if you're not honest."

"Supposing you want to do the Pennine Way again?"

"I'll have to give Horton a miss."

"That's probably a good idea," Alex said. "Have you seen *The Wicker Man*?"

We carried on up the farm track and I carried on with my lecture on the economics of the Yorkshire Dales. "My point is that they're all in it together. If you've a B&B in Blackpool and the pub on the corner is a disaster it doesn't matter. There are a thousand pubs. If you've got a B&B in Horton and the only pub in the village is ripping people off it *does* matter. In Blackpool it's every man for himself. In Horton they're a team."

"So what do you suggest?"

"I don't know. Maybe the B&Bs should have a word with the pub. Assuming they don't want vacancies on August 1st."

"But then you'd complain that the Pennine Way was crowded."

He had a point. I'm nothing if not a hypocrite. This country has an abundance of beautiful, challenging, life-changing national trails. It has an equal abundance of people who are overweight and an NHS spending a fortune on treating the consequences. I'm not suggesting that Horton-in-Ribblesdale becomes Yorkshire's answer to Machu Pichu, but we have a fantastic resource that the vast majority of people know nothing about. But as I said, I'm a hypocrite. Why do I love walking so much? Not least, because of the solitude.

You might think I've been a bit harsh on little village nestling snugly in the Yorkshire Dales. If anyone in Horton buys the book I'm unquestionably inviting a 1* review on Amazon and, yes, I'm risking *Wicker Man 2* if I ever go back. But too many travel writers – seduced by the free trip or pressured by the paper's advertising department – say everything is wonderful. If you say everything is wonderful then, ultimately, nothing is wonderful.

The Roman Road

"The map says we're on a Roman road."

"It says here it's called Cam High Road."

"Sounds like somewhere in Surrey. But all Roman roads had names. My dad insisted on calling the A5 Watling Street. And the Fosse Way. I think that went to Lincoln."

No wonder children used to get bored on long car journeys. My dad lectured me on Roman roads, I forced my children to play quizzes.

"I-Spy!" Alex shouted one day as we passed the time on the way to Leeds-Bradford airport. "Something beginning with H"

"Hedge? Horse? House?"

The four of us did our best. Two of us with degrees, one who'd go on to get a First from Cambridge, one who'd get a Masters in Marketing. But after ten minutes we were absolutely defeated.

"We give in. What is it that begins with H?"

"Tree!" Alex yelled in triumph.

He was only three at the time...

This morning's Roman road was straight – no surprise there – constantly uphill and shrouded in mist. Or maybe it was low cloud: we could see about five yards on either side.

"It makes you wonder why Hadrian bothered," I said.

"You mean why did he conquer Britain?"

"Yes."

"He didn't. Hadrian built the wall. It was Claudius that invaded."

"Then why did they come this far north? I can't believe the troops were impressed. Marching through the mist. Waiting for the Picts to appear over the hill." I pointed into the fog. "Just imagine it."

"While back in Italy they could be picking grapes on their farms..."

"Exactly."

"You've seen *Gladiator* too many times, Dad. The Roman army was mostly made up of the people they'd conquered."

That's the trouble with a son who wants to do History at university. You think you've scored a point with your rapier-like insight into the mind of the average Roman soldier and he has the audacity to reply with a fact.

"OK, I've got a question for you," I said. "How in the name of Zeus - "

"Jupiter, Dad."

"How did they walk on this? Here we are, marching uphill. We're wearing walking boots, double-layer, 1,000 mile, indestructible socks and my feet are starting to hurt on these loose stones. So how did they manage it in sandals?"

"They didn't. They wore *caligae*. Studded, heavy-soled sandals."

"What? Even in winter? They must have had an army of cobblers following them."

And as we continued trudging uphill – hopefully towards some sunshine and a view – we spent a cheerful fifteen minutes discussing the mobile shopping mall that followed the Roman legions. "Pots and pans..."

"Sword sharpeners..."

"And prostitutes," Alex said.

"Er...yes," I said. Clearly the national curriculum has moved on since I did History A-level. Were we about to spend five minutes on the sex life of the Roman soldier? Cue embarrassed parent mode.

Thankfully, no. Alex had more pressing concerns. "Is there any Kendal Mint Cake left? I think I'm developing a taste for it."

I breathed a sigh of relief: every parent of a teenager will know how I felt. I was watching TV with him. It was *Sinbad the Sailor* – he must have been 12 or 13. A slave girl fell overboard. Somehow two minutes in the sea washed all her clothes off. I squirmed in embarrassment on the sofa. Alex simply continued his relationship with Ben and Jerry's Phish Food.

The path bent round to the left. And carried on going uphill. Alex was a couple of yards in front of me now. I was starting to struggle with the pack and we hadn't stopped for lunch yet.

"Are you OK, Dad?" What was this? Telepathy? Cats were supposed to be able to sense your feelings, not teenage boys. But then Beverley had always believed in Alex's emotional intelligence.

As a small child he'd cried out in the middle of the night. As mums do she went into his room and lay down beside him, talking to him, telling him it had only been a dream, soothing him back to sleep. "I'm sorry I woke you up, Mummy," he said.

"It doesn't matter, darling," she replied, "I was awake anyway. I couldn't sleep."

"What was bothering you, Mummy?" our empathetic youngest had asked.

What was bothering his dad was the pack. I was five yards behind him now, bending further forward, staggering occasionally on the camber, concentrating on walking in the middle of the track. Today was supposed to be 13½ miles. What had we done? Seven? I fumbled for my phone. Three goes and I managed to tap 9-4-5-2 and hit Walkmeter. 6.3 miles, 2 hours 34 minutes. "Bugger," I said out loud.

"What's the matter?"

"Nothing. I'm good."

"Do you want me to take the pack?"

"No, no, I'm fine. Never better."

"You're falling behind..."

"I was just checking my phone, that's all. Let's get another mile done. Past halfway for the day then we'll have some lunch." I bent forward a few more inches and staggered drunkenly after my son.

We didn't find two conveniently flat rocks to sit on. We weren't at the top of a hill gazing down into a valley. And the sun most definitely wasn't on our faces. We stood by a gate, peered five yards into the fog and unpacked £15 worth of packed lunch.

Or at least Alex did.

I was still trying to disentangle myself from the pack. Then a figure emerged from the mist. An impossibly good-looking young man. Designer stubble, shades of Tom Hiddleston – and clearly lost on his way to a photo-shoot. "Is this the way to Hawes?" he asked.

Despite the pack I stood up straight. Obviously I looked like a proper walker: someone who could be relied on for directions. Sadly no. He was talking to Alex. Another bite taken out of my ego. "Straight on," my son replied. "Maybe six or seven miles."

And I went back to struggling with the pack. Alex had fastened it to me with so many straps, belts and buckles that I was trapped. I was also exhausted. We'd climbed over 1,000 feet that morning and – goodness knows how I'd missed it – some sadist had slipped a few extra bricks into the pack along the way. Eventually my son saw my struggles: he came over and re-leased me.

The pack slid to the floor. Mentally and physically a great weight fell from my shoulders. And I couldn't help it. I lurched forward: bounced around like an astronaut on the moon. Then I slowly re-adjusted to life as a normal human being instead of the world's oldest member of the Special Forces.

And what a reward was waiting for me. The Crown's packed lunch. Yesterday's bread, two slices of beef admittedly. But mustard? Mayonnaise? You must be joking. The bread and the margarine were on first name terms, but only just. A 500ml bottle of water and a Kit Kat. And, of course, a packet of salt n' vinegar. *Aye, Give 'em both t'salt n' vinegar, Gladys. 'Appen they'll be eight miles away by t'time they find out. They'll not be walking back to complain...*

Lunch was over. Time to walk into Hawes. I sighed and reached for the pack.

"Do you want me to carry it, Dad?"

"No," I said, fingers crossed behind my back. "You carried it yesterday. I'll carry it today. And then we'll do half and half to-morrow."

"But if you carry it for the rest of the day you won't be able to carry it tomorrow."

That was it in a nutshell. And we both knew it. There was si-lence for thirty seconds as I accepted the inevitable.

I remembered the moment – trying to move my car out of a snowdrift – when I realised it had all changed. When I realised I was responsible for my dad's health, not the other way around. I'd been about 25. It had arrived slightly earlier for Alex.

He bent forward and lifted the pack up. "Are you sure?" I asked.

"Do we want to finish?" he replied.

And we set off walking towards Hawes.

In which we meet an American

We were at the top of Sleddale Pasture, maybe two miles from Hawes, picking our way from one pile of rocks to the next. Across ground that was increasingly boggy. "How can the top of a hill be boggy?" I asked. "Why doesn't the water drain to the bottom?"

"Don't ask me," Alex said. "I'm concentrating. You need to deal with life as it is, Dad, not as you want it to be."

My son the life coach. That was me told. And whatever the reason the water hadn't drained away, so we carried on squelching from cairn to cairn through the mist and – in my case – treading very carefully. If there was one thing I was emphatically *not* going to do on this walk it was fall in a bog.

A hundred yards ahead another pair of walkers were treading just as carefully. Only one small backpack between them: a couple who'd enjoyed a leisurely breakfast in Hawes and then gone for a gentle eight or nine mile round trip. 'What an ideal holiday,' I found myself thinking. The person who used to be a fully paid-up member of the sun lounger, beer-by-the-pool club. Now the first thing I looked for was the tick box that said 'walking boots essential...'

"We're going to catch them up, Dad."

"We are. How many people is that we've seen today? Do we need two hands yet?"

We duly overhauled them. A husband and wife? She was American: he – if my accent radar was working – was from somewhere around Cambridge. And no, I know that doesn't preclude marriage, but they weren't married. Were they?

Damn it, I'm a writer. I'm supposed to be an expert on people and relationships. So were they a couple or weren't they?

He held her hand to help her over a stile. Put his hand in the small of her back. She was talking about a hiking trip in the Sierra Nevada. "You should have come with me," she said.

They both wore wedding rings. What *was* this? Discreet dating for the over-50's hill walker?

I gave up playing detective and started talking to them.

She was from California. "The Napa Valley. Wine country. Do you know it?"

No, I didn't. And as I tiptoed carefully around another bog the wineries of Napa Valley seemed about as real as Narnia.

Inspector Morse decided they were married. University lecturers, separated by careers. Still caring for each other but distantly. Neither of them seeing any need to end the relationship.

"Are you doing all of the Pennine Way?" she asked.

"We're doing five days. Around 80 miles. My wife's picking us up in Dufton. Unless she's changed her mind after a week without me."

They laughed. For some reason Alex sighed and said, "Six" under his breath.

We carried on talking as we walked down towards Hawes, Alex patiently answering the inevitable 'what are your plans?' questions.

There's no other way to put this: the Pennine Way's entry into Hawes is disappointing and slightly depressing. You've walked 14 miles through spectacular scenery – well it would have been spectacular if we could have seen it – and you end up walking into Hawes through an estate, squeezing down an alleyway between houses.

But you're in a forgiving mood. It's been a long day, the B&B isn't far away. Neither is the pub. So you'll put up with the main street, but it's an anti-climax to end the day.

And here I was, back at Herriots in Hawes. Four months after I'd paid my £20 deposit and first come face to face with the Pennine Way. Mrs Herriot was giving a long, complicated explanation about the toilet. I wasn't listening. You've walked 14 miles, you don't really want a technical explanation about a toilet. Something about water pressure? "It's going to make a noise." I got that bit.

She left us to it and Alex went to the loo. Holy Moly! The noise! The toilet was a direct descendant of the Tardis. It would be worth a fortune at a Doctor Who convention. Fortunately it kept Alex in the same dimension. I followed him, managed to avoid a day trip to Skaro and decided he'd earned the most precious gift I could give him after another day with his dad.

"Would you like some time on your own? I'll just walk up the road and have a drink at the pub. Password? It'll be *Herriots1*. Come up when you're ready, we'll find somewhere to eat."

Tuesday Night in Hawes

This wasn't right. We'd walked 14 miles across the fells in drizzle and low cloud and here were people casually sitting outside the pub enjoying the late afternoon sunshine. And catching Pokémon.

I sat equally casually outside the pub and wrote in my notebook. With a pint of Stella and – possibly for the first time in my life – some curried peanuts.

There was a stunningly attractive girl at the next table. Blonde, I-was-a-punk-10-years-ago hairstyle. Piercings. And walking boots. So much for the gnarled veterans I'd met on the Cleveland Way and Vinegar Joe: Tuesday on the Pennine Way was full of beautiful people straight out of glossy magazines. The changing demographic I'd read about was right.

She suddenly let out a cry of triumph. I looked across at her. "Sorry," she said. "I've just caught Squirtle." The summer of 2016: that's what you did. Sat outside a pub in full walking gear and tried to catch a small Pokémon that – I had to Google it – resembles a light blue turtle.

Alex arrived and we ended up eating at the Wensleydale Pantry – the perfect place to go if you look back nostalgically on school dinners. We queued up at the hatch and ordered our meal from the dinner lady. Alex had pie and chips: I made the mistake of ordering lamb. If you're on *Masterchef*, lamb is pink. If you're in Hawes, it's grey. Maybe we'll walk around France next year...

Wednesday: The Weather Forecast

Alex was still asleep. I was watching weather forecasts, desperately trying to find one that told me what I wanted to hear. *There will be some showers in Hawes around mid-morning but they will quickly give way to a fine, dry day, perfect for those of you walking to the Tan Hill Inn.*

Sadly the forecasts were unanimous. Whichever channel I was on, the message was the same. Large blue circles moved remorselessly across North Yorkshire: light blue gave way to dark blue. There would be persistent, heavy rain over the Pennine Way from ten o'clock.

The forecasts were unanimous – and they were wrong.

The rather more reliable method of looking out of the window confirmed that it was raining now. Hawes was grey, miserable and very wet.

And today was the day. The walk to Tan Hill. The drive I'd done with my wife back in April. The drive where I'd stopped the car and looked across Great Shunner Fell. At the unremitting bleakness of it. At the total lack of shelter. The drive where I'd climbed back into the car, turned the heater up and said, "We're doing it in August. It'll be fine. Keeping cool will be the problem. And I'll warn Alex about sunstroke."

I looked out of the window again. Now the water was running down the main street. This hadn't been in the plans. But at least the path across the Fell was paved. I'd looked at Google images: the path had been paved in all of them.

Time to wake Alex up. And time for me to do some shopping before breakfast.

The Little White Bus

I suspect that the packed lunch from Herriot's – if I ever write a bestseller I'll be quite irritated if an entire district rips off the name of the main character – may have been better than the first two examples of the craft, but I wasn't prepared to risk it. Besides, downpour or no downpour, I wanted variety. And there was a butcher's across the way, obligingly open at eight in the morning.

"Good morning." I said and duly bought some ham, cheese and a couple of seductive chicken and mushroom pies. After months of watching what I ate while I whittled myself down to the shape of an Olympic athlete (in the rifle shooting, probably. We're not in Mo Farah territory...) it was some consolation to know I'd be consuming so many calories today that I could buy their entire stock of seductive pies and still lose weight.

But pies were one thing. I needed information as well. "We're supposed to walk from here to Tan Hill today," I said.

Meaningful glances were exchanged behind the counter. "Today?"

"In this?"

Oh crap, not more grimp and mire.

"If it gets worse..." I gestured out of the window. "Can we get a bus from here to Tan Hill?"

"Well, there's the Little White Bus..."

The 'Little White Bus' sounded cute, but not immediately reliable. It sounded like something that turned up in your son's school bag. *What's Alex got to read tonight? Well he's finished 'The Little Blue Pirate.' Looks like it's 'The Little White Bus.'*

Or a bus service run by volunteers. *The Little White Bus is cancelled today. Arthur's taking his wife to the dentist.*

As the water cascaded down Hawes' main street I wanted to know that the 93B left at 10:17 and would arrive at Tan Hill at 11:44. What we'd do at Tan Hill for an entire afternoon was another matter, but right then it looked far less of a problem than walking there.

"Is there a timetable anywhere?"

"Outside the market."

"Where's that?"

"Right at the top of town."

So in order to find out about the Little White Bus – which I was considering so I wouldn't get soaked to the skin – I'd to have to walk all the way up the main street and get soaked to the skin. Catch-22, or whatever the equivalent is in the Yorkshire Dales.

"Thank you," I said and paid for my pies. I sprinted across the road back to the B&B. It made no difference.

"You're wet, Dad."

"No, I'm soaked. It is seriously pouring down."

"You've got your waterproof jacket."

"No, I have a golf jacket. That's all I have. We're doing this in August. Mid-summer. I didn't expect to have to bring arctic survival equipment. And by the time I'd paid for all the B&Bs I couldn't afford it. A line had to be drawn somewhere and I drew it through 'waterproof jacket for dad.' So I've got a jacket which lets in water after three shots on a golf course."

"I'll go downstairs for breakfast," my son said tactfully.

"Yeah. I'll be down in a minute. I'll give your Mum a ring."

We couldn't catch the bus, could we? However wet I was going to get, we couldn't catch the bus. *How did it go on the Pennine Way? Yeah, good. Monday we went up Pen y Ghent. Tuesday we walked to Hawes. Wednesday we caught the bus and spent the afternoon playing Monopoly.*

I watched another weather forecast and phoned my wife. And something snapped. I had a meltdown.

"You know what? I can tell you this and I can't tell Alex. It's pissing down; I don't have a waterproof jacket. I have to walk 16 or 17 miles across a moor or a fell or whatever it's called. I have to climb higher than Pen y Ghent. You want to know the truth? I'm frightened. I don't know if I can do it and I daren't tell my son that. There you are. That's the bottom line. I'm a middle aged writer who suddenly realises he knows bugger all about walking and I'm scared."

"What are you scared of?"

"I'm scared of getting soaked. I'm scared of not being able to do it. I'm scared of having to give up. But when it comes down to it what I'm really scared of is letting my son down."

And then I went downstairs for breakfast.

A small rant on the subject of breakfast

"And if you could fill in the form in your room and let us know what you'd like for breakfast," Mrs Herriot had said on Tuesday after she'd finished explaining about the time travelling toilet.

What?

Order our breakfast now? We've just walked 14 miles. I want a shower, I want a drink, I want to look at my black toenail. Much as I love breakfast, right now I have no interest in it.

So I'm very sorry, I'm going to have a small rant. The Pennine Way brought many of my food rants to the fore: microwaving baked beans, the ever-present salad garnish, the ridiculous overuse of 'award-winning.' But none more than ordering your breakfast the night before. It's like people putting the empty wrappers back in the After Eight box. It's like a footballer wearing no. 94 on his shirt. It's simply wrong.

How can you possibly order your breakfast the night before? Supposing I'd woken up early and gone for a long walk and needed more than the porridge I'd self-righteously already ordered? Supposing I'd simply gone off the idea of Eggs Benedict?

So this notion of ordering breakfast the night before needs to be resisted at all costs. I appreciate it may make Mr & Mrs B&B's life a lot easier, but it has to be stamped out. 'No, you're a B&B. I've paid my money, you've got a breakfast menu. I'm paying you for bed and breakfast. And a key part of that break-fast is choice, when I'm ready to make a choice.'

One of the pleasures of staying in a hotel or a B&B – at least for me – is coming down to breakfast and having a leisurely look at the menu, knowing you don't have to cook and you don't have to default to the same breakfast you always have.

Ordering the night before is like your wife winking at you and saying, 'The kids are all out on Friday night, let me know what position you want.' (Please note that 'slumped in front of the TV' is not the correct answer.)

The solution, I suppose, is to order a full English and leave what you don't want. Except there go the Eggs Benedict and the por-ridge. So the real answer is for B&Bs to stop this ridiculous practice and realise that choice – like perfect Wi-Fi and toilets that aren't waiting for a plumber from Gallifrey – is as impor-tant as water coming out of the taps.

King Canute

I watched our bags disappear into the back of a minibus. "You walking to Tan Hill?" the driver said.

"That's the plan."

He shook his head. "Best of luck," he said as he climbed back behind the wheel.

We walked out of Hawes. I was wearing my shorts, stupidly pinning my hopes on a tiny oasis of blue sky, the fact that – for now – it was only spitting and blind faith in every weather forecast being wrong.

We turned right and started up the hill. "Bluebell Hill, Dad," Alex said as he checked the map.

"That's nice. And it's stopped raining. I told you shorts would be fine."

"You know who you're like, Dad?"

"No, tell me."

"King Canute. You think if you put shorts on you can magically control the weather. 'Oh, it's monsoon season. Never mind, I'll put my shorts on. That'll make the sun come out.'"

Alex was right. My shorts were fine for about two hundred yards. Then I carelessly looked up to my left. The hills in the distance had disappeared. And it had started spitting again.

We were half way up the hill. The rain was getting steadily stronger. There was no alternative. It was time to admit defeat.

But at least I had a choice. I could admit defeat by putting my tail between my legs, scurrying back to Hawes and waiting for the Little White Bus.

Or I could admit that wearing shorts wasn't going to make the sun come out and do what I should have done in the B&B: put my waterproof trousers on.

But there's a significant difference between putting waterproof trousers on when you're sitting on a bed in the B&B – and putting them on halfway up a hill, trying to haul them over your boots while the rain lashes down.

I was hopping around on one leg doing some sort of idiotic quickstep. "Maybe if you undid the zips at the bottom, Dad..."

I looked around desperately – surely there must be a rock I could lean on? No. There was only my son. I didn't want to ask him for help. But the alternative was falling over. "Stand still so I can hold on to you, will you?"

Eventually I was dressed. Dressed – and committed. As we started off up the hill I realised this was it. I was saying goodbye to any thoughts of the Little White Bus. I was committing myself to 15 or 16 more miles. Committing myself to the walk across Great Shunner Fell. What had I said on that cold, crisp day in April? "It'll look different in August."

Too right it did.

The rain continued to fall and we plodded steadily uphill. My 'waterproof' golf jacket didn't let me down. Waterproof on a golf course is one thing: you've a giant umbrella and if you've any sense you're standing under a tree. Waterproof on Great Shunner Fell with absolutely no protection from low cloud, rain and – hell's teeth, now it was hailing – was another dimension. Inevitably, King Canute's jacket failed to hold back the tide.

And no, before you ask, I didn't have a hat.

And where were the paving stones? Had Google images lied to me? Path? We were walking up a stream.

No. Here they were. OK, so I was going to get wet. But I could cope with that if it was 15 miles on paving stones. Rain, low cloud, fog, even hail. I could cope if we were walking on paving stones.

They ended after 400 yards.

And that's how it was for the rest of the morning. "There's some paving stones up ahead, Dad."

"Thank God for that." Suddenly walking becomes easier, I start to relax, almost feel good despite the rain... And the paving stones end.

"Here we go again," I sigh in frustration. "Back to wading upstream."

"Dad, the paving stones aren't here to make your life easier. They're here to protect the fells against erosion."

Technically I knew Alex was right. But I couldn't shake the feeling that the sadist who'd slipped extra bricks into the backpack had a job in the National Parks office.

It's not the walking that kills 'em, Eli. It's the hope...

Tha's right there, Josiah. What do you say? Every four 'undred yards?

Aye. Just enough to make t'daft buggers think the path'll last for t'rest of t'morning...

The Teachers

Soaking wet or not I needed a wee. "I'm just going round that corner."

"OK, I'll have some of the soup."

I'd bought a flask and asked Herriot's to fill it with their carrot and coriander soup – one of the very few sensible decisions I made that day.

I went 20 yards round the corner, turned my back to the rain and started rummaging through layers of wet clothes.

I was just about to expose myself to the Yorkshire Dales when I heard a noise. Voices? Don't be ridiculous.

I finally came to a dry layer. Must be nearly there...

And there it was again. People talking. Was I hallucinating? Could the rain and the cold do that to you?

I wasn't hallucinating. I looked up and two women were walking towards me. Ten more steps and they'd have seen a sight that wasn't in the guide book. "Morning." I said, desperately trying to hide my embarrassment. "Bit wet for the time of year."

They didn't bat an eyelid. They looked like teachers who'd steered countless groups of teenagers through the Duke of Edinburgh Award.

They said 'good morning,' carried on round the bend and I returned to the call of nature.

115

"Two women just passed me," Alex said.

"You don't say," I muttered.

We caught up with them a couple of miles later. They'd stopped to have a cup of tea in one of the brief spells when the rain eased off just enough to give me a few minutes' optimism.

And then we were in one of those slightly uncomfortable periods when we weren't quite walking with them but we were close enough to talk. Eventually I gave in to temptation and asked them to take a photo of us. If the weather stayed like this, we might not see anyone else before Friday. Then we gradually let them pull away from us as they headed for Thwaite and a hot chocolate. A few weeks and they'd be back at school, telling a class of eager 15 year olds that only idiots go walking on the fells without being properly prepared. And forget to have a pee before they leave the B&B...

The Best Café in the World

'Thwaite,' the sign said.

"Thank God," I said. It was half a mile, we were walking over loose rocks – how I hated them – but at least we were coming down off Great Shunner Fell.

"Let's have some lunch," I said to Alex. "It looks like the rain's easing." It wasn't easing, it was pausing for breath and we both knew it. But you can't admit to yourself that you're going to be wet for another four hours.

There wasn't a lot to Thwaite. But there was a seat in the middle of the village. "Over there?" I said.

It seemed the only logical place. But then the drizzle turned back to serious rain.

"There's a café," Alex said.

"They won't let us in. We're soaked."

"Go and ask."

Alex collapsed onto the seat. I walked across to the Kearton Country Hotel's café. Let me offer an unbiased review: it is by some distance the best café in the world. "Do you mind if we come in?" I asked the girl behind the counter.

"Sure. Why not?"

"We're soaking."

"There's a wooden seat in the window."

A latte. A hot chocolate. A couple of biscuits. Paying meant finding the money in my shorts. I apologised to an elderly couple and – for the second time that morning – started sifting through soggy layers of clothing.

"My feet are soaking," I said, cradling my latte like the Holy Grail.

"Do you want a spare pair of socks?"

"Have you got one?"

"Of course," as if it were the most natural thing in the world. "D of E taught me to always take a spare pair of socks. Or two."

And there's a lesson for parents. You send your children to school and you tick the box that says 'music lessons' or 'swimming lessons' or 'martial arts.' There may come a time when you're invited to tick the 'Duke of Edinburgh Award' box. Sitting in the café I realised we hadn't just ticked a box with the D of E. I couldn't have made it from Hawes to Thwaite without my son. He couldn't have done it without the skills and the resilience he'd learned through the Duke of Edinburgh Award.

I took his spare socks – "You don't need to give them back to me, Dad" – and went to the toilet armed with one of our quick drying towels. But my feet were soaked. Everything was soaked.

Could I get my foot up high enough to put it under the hot air dryer? It would mean dislocating a hip but it was still tempting.

I did my best with the towel and the spare socks and went back to Alex. "It's stopped," he said.

So it had. I was reluctant to leave the café – I'll go back one day and sit nostalgically at the same table – but it was the only way to get to Tan Hill. "We'll have lunch in an hour or so shall we? In the sun, at the top of a hill."

If only...

The Bothy

I walked confidently out of the café and turned right. Alex turned left. "Are you sure?" I said. He simply stared at me. I had no map reading credits left and did as I was told.

Left it was. Through a farmyard and... down this track?

"Dad!" Not for the first time I'd walked past the signpost.

Another hill stretched in front of us, the path running diagonally across it.

After I've been back to the café I'll walk up that hill as well. Looking back towards Thwaite – even on bleak, damp day, even seeing it through intermittent drizzle, the view was beautiful. A river ran along the bottom of the valley and on a sunny day it must have been stunning.

I didn't take a photo because – hey, ho – it had started raining again. Hard. And I'd promised Alex we'd stop for lunch. We squelched through a farmyard. Maybe the farmer's wife would be at the kitchen window. Maybe she'd see us, maybe she'd have a son Alex's age, maybe she'd be moved to compassion...

Nope. None of the above. We closed her gate behind us and carried on. There was a bothy off to the right. I couldn't see a door but it most definitely had walls. We could shelter. "Come on," I said, and we paddled across the field.

"What is this?"

"I don't know. It's too big for a sheep hut. A barn? I think a 'bothy' is the technical term. Unless you're an estate agent in which case it's a prime residential site offering unrivalled views over the Dales and ripe for conversion."

"Maybe not today..."

"Maybe not. Come on, this wall looks like it'll keep us dry."

The rain was still lashing down. We were both wet and miserable. And I was feeling guilty as well. This was my son's summer holiday. This time last year he'd been in Italy sharing pizza and beer with his mates. Now he was behind a sheep hut sharing carrot and coriander soup with his dad.

Alex took the pack off and pushed his hood back. "What've we got?"

"Bread, cheese, chicken and mushroom pie."

Fresh out of the oven, plump and succulent in the butcher's, the pies had seemed a good idea at the time. Six hours later, slightly damp, they looked like... 'A challenge' is probably the kindest way to put it. Lumps of chicken in congealed soup. That black thing might just be a mushroom. Alex wisely passed. I felt morally obliged to eat at least half of one. "I'll save the rest for later," I said optimistically.

But the soup was good. The wetter I got the better it tasted. At that moment it was the best soup I'd ever had and buying the flask the most sensible decision I'd ever made. But the next hill was calling, and the rain hadn't quite made it to 'torrential,' so we set off again. "There's the path," I said. "Left at the end of the dry stone wall."

I turned left and almost trod on a grouse. Or a pheasant. I don't know. But I do know it was a female. And as she moved away from me eight or nine chicks were suddenly there.

"Alex! Look!" Suddenly I was David Attenborough. But I was David Attenborough yelling at the top of his voice instead of whispering into the camera. I was doing my absolute best to frighten the chicks away. "Let me get a photo!" Attenborough fumbled for his iPhone. Put the wrong passcode in. Put the right passcode in. Tapped photos by mistake. Said, "Shit." Closed photos and finally tapped camera.

By which time there was just one chick left.

"Nice work, Dad. Slick..."

I sighed, crossed 'wildlife photographer' off my list of potential careers and followed my son up the hill.

Frustration

It carried on raining. We carried on walking. Said, "It can't be much further," about a hundred times.

"There. That must be it." Alex is pointing at a building up ahead. It's just a grey silhouette but in this rain everything's a grey silhouette. The outline doesn't look like the Tan Hill Inn and it's up to the right. If anything, the path's heading slightly downhill. But I don't say so.

Alex is tired, frustrated, fed up. Mostly with me. God knows how he's kept going. I'm exhausted. And soaked. But the only thing to do is keep walking. Tan Hill *must* be round the next corner. We're already way over 16 miles for the day: how much further can it be?

The grey silhouette drifts past on the right. Maybe a hundred yards up the hill. Just another farm.

"Keep going," I say. "It can't be much further." A hundred and one...

Suddenly I was thirsty. I'd barely drunk any water all day – unless you count opening my mouth and catching the rain – now I finished half my water bottle in one go. Alex was five yards in front of me and I was struggling to keep up. We turned right and I stumbled up yet another long, wet hill. The gap widened to ten, then twenty yards. Frustration was driving Alex on: exhaustion was slowing me to a halt.

I drank the rest of my water and started to wonder. What would have happened if I'd been on my own? Would I have set off? Yes. Would I have carried on when we were half way up the hill? Yes, probably. Then what? Sooner or later I'd have taken a wrong turning...

It's hard, writing this months after the walk to convey how tough the day was. It was August 3rd. 160 miles away people were watching a test match. Sitting outside in shorts and t-shirts, wondering whether to have another beer before lunch time. We were walking across Great Shunner Fell in rain, gales, low cloud and hail. It was the day when my lack of preparation; when my lack of knowledge about walking, when my 'it'll be OK it's August' attitude could have had serious consequences. I'd wanted a physical challenge and the Yorkshire Dales and the weather had given me one.

A year from now it won't be so bad. I'll remember the teachers and eating lunch sheltering behind the bothy. Completely failing as a photographer. The rain will have faded, I won't remember how exhausted I was. At times as I walked across the fell, struggling to see the path, not knowing how much further there was to go, I *was* frightened. If I had done that walk on my own I'd have been a mountain rescue statistic. Or worse.

So let me set it down here. Without Alex, I would never have reached the Tan Hill Inn that day. Thanks, pal.

Welcome to Tan Hill

Finally, finally, finally, the unmistakable silhouette of the Tan Hill Inn loomed out of the fog.

"How far do you think it is, Dad?"

"Five hundred yards?"

Five hundred yards. At home that was from the cliff top to the car park. Straight into the evening sun, Pepper running ahead of me to get back to the car and her biscuit. Five minutes more and we'd be dry. And warm. A few short steps from a shower.

I never realised pushing the door of a pub open could make me so happy. The first thing I saw was our bags. The second thing I saw was people. Lots of them. Filling the bar.

Suddenly I wasn't one of the only two people in the world who'd walked from Hawes to Tan Hill that day, I was just a bloke waiting to be served at the bar. A very wet bloke, but one who'd have to wait his turn.

There was one barmaid. She was inviting someone to come behind the bar and pull his own pint. "How awesome is that?" he said to his mates. Who were all wearing North Face jackets. Yes, red ones. Alex had been right. What sort of man needs an eighty quid outdoor jacket to walk from his 4x4 to the bar? While the man in the sodden golf jacket stood and waited and felt water running down his back...

Finally. "Hi. We've got a room booked for tonight."

"Oh, OK. What name is it under?"

"Richards." The barmaid stared at a terminal for an eternity. The whole trip had been based around this booking at Tan Hill. Everywhere else there was a choice. At Tan Hill there was only the Tan Hill Inn. So I'd booked it first to make sure we got a room.

"I can't find it. Could it be under any other name?"

My heart sank. "No," I said. "I booked it ages ago. Back in April."

She peered at the terminal again. The nightmare scenario unfolded in front of me.

I'm really sorry. There must have been a mistake. We're fully booked, I'm afraid. But there's a bothy about two miles further on. Or you could camp in our field...

Turning to face my son. *I'm sorry, Alex, there's been a cock-up. We need to carry our bags to a bothy...*

"I'm very sorry, she's new." It could have been Basil talking about Manuel. A plump, smiling, middle-aged woman who knew how the booking system worked had taken over. "We're a bit disorganised. The managers did a bunk yesterday. Here it is. You're in room one."

She gave me a key. I resisted the urge to kiss her with some difficulty.

We walked through the pub's lounge – two young girls were playing Monopoly, a guy was strumming a guitar, life was normal, the hail on Great Shunner Fell didn't exist – and up to room one. There was a sign at the bottom of the stairs. 'No boots past this point.' I'm sorry, we were simply too tired.

Room one was compact. It didn't have a chair: it didn't have a TV. "Damn it," Alex said. "No trouser press."

As I said before, teenage sarcasm. Hail, hills, 8½ hours in the pouring rain: teenage sarcasm survives anything.

I slumped onto my bed. I'd never been this tired in my life. What was it? I looked at my phone: 16.95 miles. Just under 17 miles in rain, hail, gales, low cloud, through streams and across the Fell.

Hawes to Tan Hill had been the hardest physical challenge of my life. And I'd trained by waiting for the sun to come out and strolling along the beach.

"Ring the SAS," I said to Alex. "Tell them I can start on Monday."

Before he could do that my phone rang. Beverley. What time was it? Half-six. I'd told her we'd be there about five.

"Are you both OK?"

I was so tired I couldn't speak to her. I handed the phone to Alex. "Tell her I'll phone her when I've had a shower. When I can hold a conversation."

If Room 1 was compact Bathroom 1 was compact-er. I'd have struggled to get undressed at the best of times. Knackered and with my clothes sticking to me it was almost impossible. I took my glasses off and put them on the shelf. Too late I noticed that the shelf had a very definite slope. I watched helplessly as my glasses slid off the shelf and into the toilet.

But eventually I was in the shower. I stood there and let the water cascade over me. My left knee hurt. But that was it. I was exhausted. But I was here. I'd made it. The toughest physical challenge of my life. Way beyond anything I'd imagined. And I'd done it.

I was even strong enough to speak to my wife. But that was difficult...

"How are things at home?"

"Tell her I'll phone her when I've had a shower. When I can hold a conversation."

I'd had a shower. Finally, I could hold a conversation.

"How was your day?"

"Yeah. Tough. It rained all day. We were soaked. Completely soaked."

"Are you OK?"

"Yeah. I've just had a shower. Alex is having a shower. Then we'll go for something to eat…"

Five minutes later we'd finished talking – everything was OK at home, we'd run out of dog food – and I turned my phone off. And realised I was irritated by the conversation.

Not by my wife: by the impossibility of describing what we'd been through. By the fact that if someone is at home watching *House of Cards* and eating a couple of chocolate digestives there's no point trying to describe the walk across Great Shunner Fell. The fact that it was hailing in August. The absolute relief of walking into the café, of finally reaching Tan Hill. That I'd been frightened, that without Alex I wouldn't have got through the day.

You simply can't describe the sheer joy of standing under the shower at the end of the day. You can't explain the feeling as the aches and pains dissolve. The discovery that the simplest sachet of Nescafe is the best coffee you've ever had if you've walked 17 miles to drink it. That physically I'd achieved more in that one day on the Pennine Way than I had in the last five years.

What do you do if you're sailing around the world? 'Yeah, I'm in the Southern Ocean. Waves? Yeah, it's a bit choppy.' Or climbing Everest? Or –

"How's Mum?" Alex was out of the shower. And just in time to see my latest brainwave...

Custard and Ice Cream

While Alex was in the shower I'd had a moment of inspiration. I'd found the hairdryer and directed it into my left boot. Genius: our boots would be dried out in no time.

Thirty seconds later it stopped. Jesus, I thought, soaked, frozen, so knackered I can't speak and now I've broken the pub's hairdryer. The Tan Hill Inn: the only pub in the country with its own snow plough and without a hairdryer...

Nope, it had just overheated and cut out. We soon established a working relationship. The hairdryer worked for thirty seconds, then it had two minutes off. It had no impact whatsoever on our boots but I was still trying when Alex came out of the shower.

"What are you doing, Dad?"

"Drying the boots out. Or trying to. I thought I'd fill them with hot air."

"Why don't you just talk to them?"

We walked down to the bar for dinner. The gentleman in red coats had made the long and perilous journey back to their cars. Now there were thin, weather-beaten people in jeans and t-shirts. A guy was sitting cross-legged and barefoot by the fire, thawing out or drying out. The impossibly good looking one we'd seen yesterday.

"Hi," I said. "We saw you yesterday. On the path to Hawes."

My heart sank. Damn it. We hadn't been the only people in the world to walk from Hawes to Tan Hill today.

He looked up. Recognition dawned. "Have you walked from Hawes today?" he asked.

"Yes," I said. "Not the best day. What about you?"

"No. I've only come from Thwaite. I carried on yesterday." I smiled. Thwaite? Only from Thwaite? To hardened fell-walkers like us that was popping down to the corner shop. Our record was intact.

Alex and I both had 'today's pasta special.' Turned out it was Spag Bol: one of my specialities at home so I never order it when we're out, but we were in serious carbo-loading territory now. I needn't have worried: it was excellent.

"If it's not too much trouble," I heard a man at the next table say to the waitress. T-shirt, hollow cheeks, limped when he went to the bar: a serious walker. But it was the tone of voice I recognised. It was the tone of voice I used at Christmas when the girl at the perfume counter asked if I wanted it gift-wrapped. "If it's not too much trouble..."

"Something special?" I asked him.

"Custard and ice-cream," he said. His wife sighed and looked to the heavens.

"Custard *and* ice-cream with your pud? Impressive."

He shrugged. "I like them both. So I always ask..."

"And that tone of voice never fails does it? I always tell my boys there's a lot you can achieve by playing the 'pathetic man' card." Alex looked predictably embarrassed.

"Been far today?" he asked.

"Hawes to Tan Hill."

I don't have a tattoo. But I was beginning to see the attraction of *Hawes to Tan Hill 3.8.16.* Possibly on my forehead...

"Not bad," he said grudgingly.

But he was a Yorkshireman. He had to go one better. "Cycled across Yorkshire last week," he said.

"Impressive," I said. "That's a long way. What, Skipton to Scarborough?"

He puffed his chest out. "Settle to Filey," he said. "And back. All in one day."

It was Monty Python's *Four Yorkshiremen* all over again. And for a second I was tempted. 'Settle to Filey? Child's play. Carlisle to Copenhagen for me. With a flat tyre. *And* towing t'wife in a trailer...'

But I gave him his moment of glory. And made a mental note to add custard and ice-cream to my training regime.

Thursday: Poached Eggs for Breakfast

Thursday morning – and the day got off to the best possible start. I had a shower without needing to retrieve my glasses from the toilet.

And the rain had stopped. There was even a glimmer of sunshine. I arranged both pairs of boots on the window sill and we went downstairs for breakfast – not forgetting to say 'good morning' to our old friend from last night, the *Strictly no boots* sign.

Breakfast at the Tan Hill Inn was an exclusive club. Just the two of us and a hopefully-thawed-out-by-now Simon the male model. We'd finally introduced ourselves. But Custard-and-Ice-Cream was nowhere to be seen. He must have strapped his wife to his back and cycled home to Settle.

An exclusive club, but one that was going to be hungry.

"Do any of you have a lighter?"

Louise, the landlady, stuck her head round the door. "Sorry, no," I said, answering for both of us. Simon shook his head.

"Bugger," Louise said.

"What's the problem?"

"The chef hasn't turned up. I can't find any matches. I can't light the range and you lot want breakfast."

Her husband wandered in, wearing that triumphant look married men have when they've finally been useful. He was proudly carrying an electronic taper, or whatever they're called. You turn the gas on, pray that the local news isn't going to lead with the word 'explosion' and click the taper. Clearly it worked: Louise – visibly relieved – asked for our orders.

Alex had a full English. But I knew I'd found a kindred spirit. "To be honest, Louise, I'd just like a bloody big pile of bacon, tomatoes and toast. I'm seriously short of a bacon sandwich."

She winked at me. In another life...

And then she turned to Simon.

"Could I have a couple of poached eggs, please?"

I have never, ever, felt such empathy for another human being as I did at that moment.

If a picture's worth a thousand words the expression that crossed Louise's face was worth a million. Simon, in his beautiful, well-educated, clearly-my-family-have-money voice asking for 'a couple of poached eggs.' Obviously he'd eaten poached eggs all over the world. Obviously Michelin starred chefs had served him perfect poached eggs. But – just like me – Louise had watched Delia say simmer for one minute (a timer is essential) and then let the eggs sit in the hot water for ten minutes. She'd listened to what Jamie had to say: a pinch of sea salt, an *organic* egg and two to four minutes. And then along comes Tom bloody Kerridge and says turn the heat off and leave them for four to five minutes.

Like me she'd tried every method there was to make a perfect poached egg. And none of them had worked.

And this morning there's no chef and she can't even light the range until her husband shows up looking like a dog with two dicks and now there's this guy straight off the cover of *GQ* asking for a couple of perfectly poached eggs.

"Oh, for fuck's sake," she said.

No, that is not quite the response you'll be taught at Les Roches International School of Hotel Management, nestled snugly in the Swiss canton of Valais. But it is the reason I absolutely, unreservedly recommend you visit the Tan Hill Inn, nestled not-at-all-snugly on top of a rainswept Yorkshire moor.

But Simon was nothing if not a gentleman. "If it's a problem," he said gently, "I'll have fried."

Half an hour later we paid the bill and set off. Or rather, we didn't pay the bill. Because the sudden flight of the managers had left Louise with a problem. She didn't know how to operate the online payments system. After five minutes of trying to log in and listening to useless suggestions from me she gave up. "Can I trust you?" she said.

"Yes," I said. "You can."

"I'm going to work the bloody system out and then I'll ring you."

"OK, that's fine." And I wrote my name, address and phone number in the book – "And there's my website so you can see

I'm a proper person." We smiled at each other: I would have kissed her but there was a wall of Theakston's beer pumps between us. So that was that: time for day four. Next stop, Middleton-in-Teesdale.

"Out of the door and turn left." After Tuesday's disaster I'd spent thirty minutes with the map to make that simple decision.

"And then we should go on the road," Alex said.

"No, I've studied the map. We go straight across the moor. Or the fell. Or whatever it's called this morning."

"Not unless you want to sink, Dad. I was talking to Louise's husband. He says it'll be too boggy after the rain."

We needed to walk a mile and a half down the road and find a blue sign. A path would take us back onto the Pennine Way and we'd miss the worst of the bog. I didn't need any convincing.

How long is polite?

"That's the bloke from breakfast isn't it?" Alex said as we walked down the road.

There was a solitary walker coming towards us. "Simon? The one that wanted the poached eggs? Yes, it is."

He'd set off ten minutes before us. Now he was coming back towards us. "I'm looking for a blue sign," he said.

"Aren't we all? Apparently it's about a mile and half." I checked my watch. "So we're maybe thirty minutes from it at this speed." And with that our father/son expedition became a father/son plus guest expedition.

And I started to worry. I knew that Simon was going to Middleton. So were we. Did that mean we were obliged to spend the day with him? Was there an unofficial 'code of politeness' for walkers? Was half a mile in someone's company acceptable before you went your separate ways or one of you stopped for a tactical cup of tea?

But I had more important things to worry about. I turned around and there was a huge black cloud over the Tan Hill Inn. Either the chef still hadn't turned up or it was going to pour down. This time I remembered to unzip my waterproof trousers before I put them on. But my heart was sinking. I simply couldn't face another day of being soaked. Especially if we had company.

I needn't have worried. It rained for ten minutes – enough to soak through to my t-shirt, obviously – but then the sun came out. And we were talking about Italy.

"I walked from Bologna to Florence last year," Simon said.

Bologna? Wasn't that the gastronomic capital of Italy? As we trudged through a mixture of bogs and cow-pats Bologna to Florence seemed a rather more attractive option.

"How long did it take you?"

"Ten days. It was fantastic. Villages that hadn't changed since the Second World War. One with a huge basket of allied bombs in the main square. And the food was amazing."

Yes, I was looking forward to yesterday's chicken and mushroom soup pie.

Simon stayed with us for half an hour – so maybe there was a walkers' code of conduct. Then he announced that he wanted to press on and we stopped for a no-longer-tactical cup of tea: the last one in North Yorkshire before we crossed the border into foreign lands...

Dead Rabbits Underpass

I went off to have a wee – for once without an audience – while Alex contemplated the world with a cup of tea.

"I've just completed a full set, Dad," he said as I came back.

"Huh? What set?"

"Rabbits. On this walk I've seen every possible stage of dead rabbits. Squashed by a tractor, eaten by something large and hungry, decomposing since the Middle Ages. And now one's just died in front of me."

"What, just now?"

"Yep. Hopped up, looked at me, fell over and died."

Blimey. Had my son developed some sort of sinister superpower? Or had the poor boy been traumatised? Certainly not the latter. "Did you steal the biscuits from the bedroom?"

Alex had a reviving shortbread while I drank some tea. "This tea tastes of carrot and coriander," I said.

"I thought it tasted funny. Did you rinse the flask?"

"I can't remember. I was concentrating on making sure my glasses didn't slide into the toilet."

A year on and tea from that flask *still* tastes vaguely of carrot and coriander. Or maybe it's psychological: a permanent taste of Hawes to Tan Hill that I'll take to my grave.

We packed up, recited a brief eulogy over the recently departed rabbit and set off to cross the border. We were leaving Yorkshire. Time to go under the A66 and into County Durham.

I've always liked South Durham. We'd drive through it with the children when we were going up to Scotland on holiday, or making a return visit to the Old Country Chapel. Or we'd drive across the A66 on our way to Center Parcs at Whinfell Forest, the children getting more animated with every passing mile.

Now here we were, back in the Land of the Prince Bishops, walking through the underpass – which seemed to be doubling up as the corporation tip – and into Durham.

And also at the official half-way point for anyone doing the full Pennine Way. There was a sign on a gate to mark the fact: it had clearly been left by one of the country's leading sports psychologists: *Congratulations on completing half of the Pennine Way. Good luck with the rest, suckers.*

Into Durham and not much changed to begin with: around the occasional bog and steadily uphill through Deep Dale. But the sun was out, I was dry, I had my shorts on, life was good. And then gradually we noticed a significant difference between North Yorkshire and South Durham.

"Is it me?" I said. "Or are these stiles much harder to climb over than the ones in Yorkshire?"

"I don't know. I hadn't noticed."

"That's the joy of being young and fit. But take that one back there. Three stone steps up to it. And then double iron bars on the top."

"If you say so..."

"And the one we've just crossed. One of the steps was missing and the bars were rusty."

"Maybe there's an evil landowner, Dad. Maybe he just doesn't like walkers."

Or maybe the farmers of South Durham were in competition. That would make 'best in show' interesting at the annual gala...

What've you got this year then?

Slippery steps, iron bar at t'top. Won it for me last year.

Pah! You need to keep up with modern technology, Bert. Three steps, middle step missing. Double iron bar on top – rusty, so silly buggers in shorts spend all afternoon worrying about tetanus – and Daisy specially trained to crap exactly where they put their foot down.

There's a serious point here and it takes me back to Horton. Not for one second am I suggesting that the Pennine Way should be 267 miles of paving stones with a Costa Coffee every three miles. I am suggesting that getting people out into the countryside may not be a bad idea. And yes, I am well aware that spending a couple of hundred quid to replace a stile may be a long way down a farmer's priority list, but farming – especially hill farming – cannot be an easy way to earn a fairly meagre living. Yes, I'm sure some walkers are a bloody nuisance, leaving gates open and dropping plastic bags. But they also inject a lot of money into local economies and I suspect they could inject a great deal more. The first week in August and Alex and I more or less had the Pennine Way to ourselves. None of the B&Bs we stayed in were full. 'Untapped potential' is the understatement of the year.

Rant over. And we were coming down off Cotherstone Moor. "Half an hour more and then some lunch?"

"Sure."

Half an hour later there were suddenly three or four paths in front of us.

"Which way now?" I asked.

Alex stared at the map. "We need to keep that reservoir on our right..."

So we turned left onto what had once been a road, but was now nothing more than a track leading to a farm. 'Dead end' a sign said as we approached the farm.

"So where's the path?"

There was a dry stone wall to our left, curving round the outside of a field. Did the path follow the wall? Possibly, assuming you could get across that little pond. Alex peered at the map again. "It's definitely not back to the right."

"And that just goes into a farmyard. And it definitely says 'dead end.' And that field in front of the farm is fenced off..."

For the first time in four days I simply had no idea where we were going. It *had* to be along the side of the dry stone wall. "Sherlock Holmes, Alex," I said. "When you've ruled out everything else what's left is the truth. It's along the side of that dry stone wall. You stay there, son. I'll find the way."

I carefully jumped from rock to rock across the pond. Climbed the bank up the other side. Followed the wall round to the right. And came to another wall. A total dead end. The sheep didn't even bother running away from me. *It's alright, lads. No-one this stupid can be a threat to us...*

I turned around. Jumped even more carefully from rock to rock. No point compounding the error by spending lunchtime in a pond. Alex was leaning nonchalantly on the farm gate. "Through here," he said. "There's the sign." So it was. High up in a tree: weathered so much it was almost unreadable.

I'll never be a real walker until I get used to walking through someone's front garden – and that's the answer to my little rant, isn't it? If I were a farmer I'd soon be fairly irritated by a steady stream of people walking through my farmyard. None of them are ever going to spend any money with me, one in ten is going to leave the gate open. *Repair the stile, love? No, it'll be fine for another year. Besides, it's rusting nicely...*

The Vision

We had lunch sitting by the black waters of the appropriately-named Blackton Reservoir. Yesterday's bread and cheese and – here it was again – the chicken and mushroom pie, making more comebacks than Mickey Rourke.

Like the man you married thirty years ago the pie was starting to sag. There were definite flecks of grey. But we were hungry...

Not that hungry. I managed a mouthful and threw it into the reservoir. It sank like a stone.

"You should have asked Louise for a packed lunch."

"What? After the way she reacted to the poached eggs? I don't have enough life cover."

We finished the bread and cheese, agreed that ... you know ... once you got used to it ... carrot and coriander tea wasn't that bad... And set off for the afternoon.

We walked through another field. Another flock of sheep ran away from us. "It's not a great defence mechanism, is it?" I said.

"What?"

"Running away," I said. "Running away is fine if you're a gazelle, but if you can only run as fast as a sheep it's not really fit for purpose."

"What do you want, Dad? Sheep with spines on their back? Sheep with poisonous venom? Besides," Alex added, "It's all relative."

"What do you mean?"

"Well, if we went round the next corner and met a bear - "

"Like if a farmer decided a rusty stile with a step missing wasn't enough?"

Alex ignored my helpful intervention. "I don't need to run fast. I only need to run faster than you."

"Aren't you forgetting my athletic prowess?"

"Dad, I've seen you tear your hamstring racing Eleanor up a sand-dune. Besides, you're my dad. You'd sacrifice yourself. You can't go home to mum and say, 'I'm sorry, Bev. Our son was eaten by a bear because he couldn't run as fast as me.'"

"Isn't this all getting a bit hypothetical?"

But that's what I've always loved about my conversations with Alex. He's prepared to wander down any hypothetical side road with me, just to see where it leads. As I'm editing this page it's exactly a week until he starts at Edinburgh University: a new chapter in his life and one he's absolutely ready for. But I shall miss him so much.

I was still mulling over the best tactics to escape from a bear when it happened.

I had a vision. For a split second, a religious experience.

That's the only way to describe it.

Not quite St Paul on the Road to Damascus, but not far off. Alex was ten yards in front of me, I was alternating between the path and the long grass at the side, whichever was the dryer.

And suddenly I saw a glass hovering in the air. It was two, maybe three yards in front of me: a continental lager glass. I could see the name written on it in an old, Germanic font – something like Warsteiner. It was cold – cold like a glass of beer can only be in a hot country. I could see the beads of condensation on the glass, running down the outside...

Oh God, this was going to taste so good.

A slightly salty tang came into my mouth. As though I'd eaten two or three hand-made crisps. Or some feta cheese. Maybe with some olives...

And it was a pint. What was it you said at the beach bar in Spain? *Si, una cerveza grande, por favor.* I could feel the sun on my back: see my sun lounger.

More condensation ran down the glass. The salty tang came again. I could taste the first sip. I reached my hand out...

"Careful, Dad, there's some cow shit up ahead."

The beer vanished. The sun lounger disappeared. I was back in County Durham. Back jumping across streams that had once been paths. Back climbing over Bert's triple-barred, going-rusty, step-missing stiles.

But there were no bears. I didn't have to race my son for survival...

Dressed for the Dining Room

Coming down off Crossthwaite Common into Middleton-in-Teesdale was like flying back into Leeds-Bradford airport. We started the descent about an hour before we landed, somewhere around Birmingham. "That's Middleton down there."

"Yeah, I know."

"So why are we going up again?"

"Don't ask me. We're on the right path."

Eventually we were cleared for landing. We walked across a field, Alex pushed open a gate and we were in Middleton. "Did you see the sign on that gate?" he said.

"No, what did it say?"

"Beware of the bull."

I shrugged. "There wasn't one. We survived." The Pennine Way does that to you. By the end of the day you don't care. Bulls, bogs, beer glasses, they're all the same. The only way you're going to reach the B&B and the shower is to walk through them or around them so you may as well get on with it. But it was still good to see 'beware of the bull' as we were closing the gate...

As we walked into Middleton there was a sign just before the cattle market. 'Pennine Way,' pointing very clearly across a field. "That's saved you thirty minutes with the map tomorrow morning, Dad."

We passed a butcher's on the main street. "Another chicken and mushroom pie?" I offered. "They're bound to be open at eight."

Alex didn't reply. I took it as a sign to order two packed lunches.

Five minutes later we reached Brunswick House – easily the best of the B&Bs we stayed at. We marvelled at our room. A TV, a shelf that didn't tip everything into the toilet – and a toilet that flushed without making me think wistfully of Billie Piper.

"Still no trouser press, Dad."

"You can't have everything in life, son..."

An hour later and it was time for dinner. Our last one together: tomorrow we'd be back home. Memo to self: buy Alex some steak if you're strong enough to go to the butcher's.

The Forrester's was two doors up from the B&B. Maybe not: the impenetrable fog of cigarette smoke coming from the tables outside wasn't the best advert.

"Fish and chips?" I offered. "It's got tables outside."

"We can do better than that, Dad."

We could. We crossed the road to the Teesdale Hotel.

"Can I have a ginger beer?" the guy in front us at the bar was asking. I've always admired people who drink ginger beer – a sure sign that they grew up reading Enid Blyton's *Famous Five*.

While Dick (or Julian) was ordering his drinks I looked around for a menu. "What do you think?" I said. "Another curry the dog would reject?"

"Maybe..."

"I mean damn it, just once I'd like something more than award-winning sausages, curried leftovers or battleship grey lamb."

"You're probably right..."

"Alex. Are you paying attention to me? Stop staring over my shoulder."

"How about some humble pie, Dad?" Alex was staring over my shoulder at the menu. At the extensive menu. Or whatever comes after 'extensive.' Writ large on an enormous blackboard over the fireplace. Scallops, Sausage and Black Pudding Scotch Egg, Steak and Black Sheep Ale Pie: my heart soared.

But first we needed a drink. "Let's sit out the front and watch the world go by," I said. "Catch the last of the sun."

The world didn't go by. But plenty of heavy lorries did, and the sun swiftly went behind a cloud. So we were back paying homage to the menu before you could say 'diesel fumes.'

Twice-baked Blue Wensleydale Soufflé, Smoked Local Trout, Sea Bream... If you're a foodie and you're walking the Pennine Way I'd recommend a route that passes the Teesdale Hotel three or four times.

"Are we going to eat in the dining room?"

"We're not dressed for the dining room are we?"

"Damn it, Dad. We've walked 70 miles. That must qualify us for a comfy chair and a table."

And like the café in Thwaite, they didn't mind at all. Steak for Alex, the Teesdale Burger for me and the dining room it was.

...Complete with some truly outstanding décor. Think 1950s cruise liner. A long thin room that's missing its role in life if the freemasons of Middleton-in-Teesdale don't meet there on the first and third Tuesday of every month.

But the burger was excellent. Local lamb topped with Teesdale blue cheese, big fat onion rings and served on a wooden board. Yes, I admit it. I like my food on lumps of oak and chunks of slate. My favourite 'plate' at home is part of an old oak barrel. Sadly I've not yet had a full English breakfast served on a shovel: I can only apologise for that gap in my CV.

"Are you doing the Pennine Way?" a lady at the next table asked.

"Some of it," I said. "We finish tomorrow. My wife's picking us up in Dufton. Unless she's changed her mind after a week without me."

They dutifully laughed. I saw Alex out of the corner of my eye. What was that expression on his face? He looked as though he was in pain...

"You know you've said that to everyone we've met, don't you?" he said as we walked back to the B&B. "You've told it about 20 times and I've had to listen every time."

"I know. But when a joke works I'm unwilling to desert it."

"Unwilling? I think you mean 'unable...' You're clinically addicted to that joke, Dad."

Friday: Ferns, Photos, More Frustration

Just like the Priory in Middleham, I could have lingered over breakfast at Brunswick House. By some distance it was the best breakfast we had. Black treacle cured bacon and the poached eggs Simon ordered. Toast that had been on intimate terms with the toaster. Yoghurt and continental cheeses if you were so inclined. A selection of bread. And a homemade fruit loaf. After four days of walking, I could have stayed in that dining room for some time. Reading the paper, re-filling my coffee, maybe just one more slice of toast...

But the Pennine Way was calling: our last and longest day. Middleton-in-Teesdale to Dufton. About 20 miles – and we'd an appointment to keep. "We'll meet Mum around five o'clock," I said to Alex. "Five-thirty at the latest. Let's go."

We paid the bill, put the bags in the front hall and shook hands.

"My wife will be here for the bags about three o'clock," I said.

"And then she's picking you up in Dufton?"

"Unless she's changed her mind about him over the last week," Alex said before I could open my mouth.

Disappointingly, the owner of Brunswick House laughed out loud.

I put the theft of my joke behind me and we set off. The sun was shining, the birds were singing and the butcher's was resolutely shut.

"So we'd have been pie-less, Dad." We would. Another tick in Alex's column.

We turned right at the cattle market and walked serenely through a field. How easy was this?

"It's a bit wet," Alex said.

"Yeah, must have rained last night. But this is easy. 20 miles like this and we'll be sitting in the café waiting for Mum..."

My optimism lasted for a mile. We climbed over another stile – three steps, no bars: they were breaking us in gently this morning – and headed towards the river. And suddenly it was loose rocks underfoot and wading through ferns. 'Wading' being the operative word.

One of us had decided on long trousers and was dry – and smug. One of us had opted for his shorts and was getting wet. Very wet, very quickly.

"My shorts are soaked. They're wet through from the ferns."

"Your choice, Dad. You'll have to live with the consequences." Sympathy was non-existent. Alex marched ahead, clearly determined to reach Dufton by lunchtime.

Another stile. And we were back in the real world. Slippery steps, double bar on the top and if you missed your footing and tripped you'd roll straight down a slope into the River Tees.

"Soaking wet ferns, loose rocks, killer stiles. It's like Dr. bloody No."

"What are you talking about, Dad?"

"James Bond, Dr. No," I shouted at my son's increasingly distant back. "He has to climb up a tube, through some tarantulas, then the tube gets hot - "

"It gets hot? That's hardly a problem is it? Achtung, Mr. Bond. Ve are going to make it pleasantly warm for you."

"Dr. No was Chinese..." But he was away. Blofeld was in the South of France inviting Bond to lie by the pool. "Und maybe ze martini, Bond? No-one can resist."

Another essential part of parenting where I'd failed. Alex's knowledge of early Bond villains simply wasn't good enough.

"How does he die, Dad?"

"Dr. No? Bond dumps three tons of bird shit on his head."

We came to Low Force and then – not surprisingly – High Force, two impressive waterfalls that demanded I took photos.

"Take a few of me on these rocks, will you?" I said.

"Don't you think your Twitter followers have better things to look at, Dad?"

Alex was getting frustrated with me, worrying about getting to Dufton on time. "Look," I said. "We set off at eight. It's twenty miles. We go at 2½ miles an hour. Eight hours. That takes us to four. Add on an hour for lunch. Maximum. Thirty minutes for breaks. We'll be there around 5:30. There aren't going to be any problems."

How could there be? Now we were walking along a neatly ordered footpath through the Raby Estates, the Tees on our right. If you're reading this, Lord Barnard, it was a pleasure to walk through your land. The path, the information boards, the lack of rusty stiles. Could I suggest a quiet word with one or two of your neighbours?

As we walked uphill after High Force I looked back at the valley and continued my love affair with the North Yorkshire/South Durham countryside. The rolling hills, the Tees running along the bottom, white farmhouses dotted in the distance. I realised I was feeling nostalgic: not for Teesdale, but for the walk. 15 miles to go, but it ended today. And we were on the home stretch. Nothing could go wrong now.

I realised something else as well. There were 15 miles to go and I'd inwardly shrugged and thought, 'So what?' Six months ago I'd seen four miles with the dog as a once in a lifetime expedition. I'd come a long way...

"We Should Talk About This..."

"We should talk about this," I said as we continued our serene progress along the river bank.

"What do you mean?"

"Public speaking. People would like the story. Father/son. What went right, what went wrong. What we learned about each other."

"I learned that you can't read a map."

"It would be funny. But moving at the same time."

"I thought you were going to write a book?"

"Yeah. I am. But I've never spoken in public with you. It's on my bucket list."

Maybe I should explain...

I've always enjoyed public speaking. That's not a statement many people can make. And you've been reading the book long enough now to know there are plenty of things I *can't* do, so let me mention one thing I can do: write speeches. It's a small part of my 'day job.' I wish I did more of it.

So when I stand up to speak in public, I know I'm armed with a good speech. And I'm a more than competent speaker. I am not, however, as good as my son. He has natural empathy with an audience; I don't.

"Ms Powell grabbed me in English," Alex said one night when he'd just turned 14.

"What did she want?"

"She says I've volunteered to give the vote of thanks in the school public speaking competition."

"That's good. When is it?"

He told me. "OK. Two weeks. That's not a problem."

I set to work on his speech and – just as we'd done before – we rehearsed it together. I count myself very fortunate: all my three children have given me some very special moments. But one of my happiest memories as a dad – one of the great joys of my life – has been rehearsing with Alex.

When Alex was seven he was the *Grumpy Innkeeper* in the school nativity play of the same name. Aged 10 he was Scrooge in *A Christmas Carol*. Alex is dyslexic – and he's a long way up the scale – so when he was younger he couldn't learn his lines by reading them. We'd lie on the bed night after night, scripts in front of us, going through his lines time after time. I was Mary, I was Joseph, I was Bob Cratchit, the Ghost of Christmas Past, Present and Future – and by the time we'd finished we both knew the play off by heart.

So when I said 'we should talk about it' I knew I was pushing at an open door. And I was being selfish: I wanted to rehearse with him one last time.

"Where do we go now?" Suddenly there was a road in front of us.

"Let me look at the map," Alex said. "Sayer Hill? New House?"

"I don't know. We go on the road for a hundred yards or so don't we?"

"Then can we stop for lunch?"

"I hope so. I'm tired."

"Yeah. Me too..."

Falling...

Maybe we *were* tired. Maybe we just weren't concentrating. Maybe the sun was shining, maybe we were thinking about going home. Whatever the reason, we decided to climb over a gate.

"We haven't had to climb a gate before have we?"

"I don't think so. Maybe it's locked for a reason, Dad. The farmer's prize bull – moved here from Middleton."

"We'll risk it. I know you want to get home. Come on, we've made good time this morning."

We climbed over the gate and walked along what looked like an abandoned railway platform. "How are you feeling?" I asked Alex.

"I'm OK. What about you?"

"Not bad. I'm tired. Five days was about right. But this has been a lovely last day. Sun shining, easy walking."

"I'm looking forward to my own bed," Alex said. He was too polite to add, 'And my dad not snoring next to me.'

The platform petered out. We went through a gap in a wall and into a field. The river was on our left, but we were gradually moving away from it.

"I thought we were supposed to stay by the river?"

"Not always," Alex said. "We'll get back to it."

Suddenly the grass was becoming longer, the track more difficult to see. Now the grass was up to our knees. It was that tough, clingy grass you get near boggy ground.

Alex stopped and looked at the map. "Are you sure this is right?" I said. "Weren't we supposed to walk along a road for a hundred yards or so?"

"There's a road up there."

So there was. A delivery van trundled along it.

But it was 400 yards uphill. This *couldn't* be the Pennine Way. We'd never been in grass this thick. There was no path. Just the road to our right and a farmhouse maybe half a mile in front of us.

"Do you think we should get to that farmhouse and ask for directions?"

The wrong thing to say. "We don't need to ask directions do we, Dad? We've got the map."

"Well the map doesn't say anything about us being stuck in the middle of a field does it? And there's another problem. I'm starting to sink."

"I'm going up to that road."

"Damn it, Alex. That road *can't* be right. We're supposed to stay by the river."

"Well what do you suggest?"

"I don't know. Walk down to the river. Maybe we should be on the other side."

"That means walking back a mile. How much time are we going to lose?"

"Well maybe we can get across the river..."

"Don't be stupid, Dad."

We were close to falling out. For the first time in five days. We'd made a mistake: we had to go back to the road. But I didn't want to say it. I didn't want to undermine Alex. He didn't want to admit he might be wrong. So we were standing in a boggy field with grass up to our knees. And I was still sinking.

"If we go down to the river we have to get over that wall."

"Well that's another sign we're lost isn't it? There's always been a stile. Now there isn't."

We stood in silence for another minute, the goodwill, the camaraderie, the friendship of the last four days rapidly evaporating.

"Come on," I said. "Let's get over that wall."

We waded downhill. I could hear the clock ticking, feel Alex's frustration. We were supposed to be in Dufton by five o'clock. We weren't going to be anywhere near Dufton by five o'clock.

The wall was waist high. A traditional dry stone wall – and definitely no stile. I peered over to the other side. If anything the ground looked even boggier. Slightly ashamed of myself I took a loose stone off the top of the wall and threw it on the ground. "Something to step onto," I said in my defence.

I'm not the most athletic of climbers. Gates, walls, I don't do any of them elegantly. But I made it to the other side without any damage.

"More grass," Alex said as he joined me. "And then a river we can't cross. I'm going back to the road." He turned around, ready to climb back over the wall.

"Fuck it, Alex, no. The road is wrong. It's four hundred yards uphill through a bog and in the wrong direction."

Bang. The first argument of the week. The first time I'd sworn at him. Tiredness, frustration, not knowing what the hell I was looking at when I looked at a map. The fear of being lost. They'd all got the better of me.

"I'm going down to the river," I snapped. "Just follow me."

And I set off. Started to walk more and more quickly. Trying to run. Trying to find out where we were and how to get back on track. Trying to run the frustration off. There was no path. All I could do was keep going downhill, jumping from one patch of grass that didn't look like a bog to the next.

"Careful, Dad," I heard Alex shout behind me.

Too late...

My right foot went straight through the grass. Suddenly I was trying to walk on water. It flooded into my boot. Momentum carried me forward. I twisted as I fell.

The top half of me landed on firm ground. From the waist down I was in a bog.

"Dad? Are you alright?"

"I'm soaked..."

"Your phone!" Alex suddenly shouted.

The impact had knocked it out of my pocket. I must have looked ridiculous. A grey-haired bloke in a bog searching frantically for his iPhone. But it had all the photos. I sprawled over and grabbed it.

"Are you sure you're alright, Dad?"

"No. I'm soaked. I'm completely bloody soaked. But I'm OK. And I'm still right."

And I stalked off down the hill again, the anger, the frustration, the embarrassment giving me new energy.

And finally I came to the river. Chances of getting across it? Not even nil. So I turned left. And saw a path. I started to walk back the way we'd come. What were we going to lose? An hour? An hour and a half? I squelched along the path. My boots were soaking. My socks were soaking. My feet were soaking. My shorts. Even my underpants.

What a bloody cock-up.

I glanced behind me. Alex was following me. Maybe a hundred yards behind me. 4½ days of getting on perfectly, of the best father/son time of my life. And we blow it on the last day. Why didn't I just reason with him? Why did I stalk off? Why are all my children so bloody stubborn?

Or maybe the question should be, 'Who's the adult here?' We weren't going to lose an hour and a half. Right now we were going to lose five days of memories.

I was back at the road. I turned right and walked over a bridge. And there it was. A sign. Public footpath. Pennine Way.

Alex caught up with me. I could see the tears in his eyes.

Only another parent will know how deeply wretched I felt at that moment.

"I'm sorry," he said.

"Oh, Christ. Nowhere near as sorry as I am. Come here."

We stood by the side of the road and hugged for a long time. I held him tightly, fiercely. Or at least as fiercely as you can when you're trying to get your arms around your son *and* a backpack.

"You're wet," Alex said.

"No, I'm not, I'm drenched. I might as well have jumped in the river."

"We've lost a lot of time."

I shrugged. "Yes we have. But so what? We were always going to get lost once in the five days. Besides," I said, "Any fool can turn up on time. Where's the drama in that?"

I pointed towards the path. "There are a couple of rocks just through the gate. We might as well have lunch while I try to dry out. And I'm sorry. Again. I shouldn't have stormed off."

"Me too. I should have known I was wrong about the road." Who's the adult here? We'd just found out.

We hugged again. "Come on," I said. Let's have lunch. Then we'll go and find your mum. But..."

"What?"

"I just need to get undressed first..."

Falling. Again...

I sat on a towel and ate a cheese sandwich. My shorts fluttered proudly in the breeze, hanging from a rusty gate.

"You're going to put your shorts back on before we start walking aren't you?"

"I've going to put my boots back on. And those spare socks you had the good sense to pack. But the answer to your question is no. If I walk a mile in my pants everything will dry out."

Alex looked doubtful, but he didn't say anything. What a star: his brother and sister would both have phoned for a taxi. And a social worker...

"Come on then," I said five minutes later. "Let's do this. It all looks straightforward now."

"You're definitely not going to put your shorts back on?"

"No."

"Can I walk in front of you then?"

"In a minute. First you have to stand there and take a picture of my bum."

"Do I have to?"

"Yes. It'll look good in the book. And art always involves suffering..."

Alex – to his eternal credit – dutifully recorded my posterior for posterity. Then he asked a sensible question. "Supposing we pass someone?"

"We won't. We haven't seen anyone for five miles."

Two minutes later a Land Rover pulled out of a farmhouse and headed down the track towards us."

"Quick, Dad!"

"Alex, we've got lost. I've fallen in a bog. We've told Mum five o'clock and we won't be there until seven. A farmer's wife seeing me in my underpants is the least of my worries. Besides," I said, "A lonely life out here on the fells, a bronzed hunk striding towards her in his best pants. She'll think it's her birthday."

The Land Rover swept past in a cloud of dust. "She didn't bother looking," Alex said.

Half an hour later I was finally dry – and to Alex's relief, fully-clothed. The sun was still shining and we were walking by the side of the Tees, hills rising on both sides of us. Malhamdale, Ribblesdale, all the other 'dales' we'd walked through... But Teesdale was my favourite. The countryside was softer, gentler, more welcoming. I felt the sun on my face and knew we were nearly home.

All we had to do now was keep walking. Sure we'd be late, but we'd get there. 5 days, what looked like it would be nearly 90 miles. And I'd done it. One argument, one plunge into a bog but otherwise five brilliant days.

There were three people up ahead. Mum, dad and their son. What would he be? About 11? 'Stephen' I heard the mum say as we got closer to them.

We were walking slightly quicker than they were. But not that much, so we had one of those conversations-while-overtaking.

"Good afternoon," I said.

"Good job you've put your shorts back on," a voice at the side of me muttered.

They were from Devon. Camping in the area for a week. It wasn't the first time they'd been to the Tees Valley. Mum had the knee support to end all knee supports. It was impossible not to ask.

"That's impressive," I said. "What did you do?"

"Oh, nothing much. Tore some ligaments water skiing."

So much for sliding gracefully into a bog and scrambling around for your iPhone.

Alex and I were in front of his parents now, but Stephen was still by my side. "We're climbing Cauldron Snout," he said. "Are you doing that?"

"If it's between us and Dufton, yes we are."

"It's the longest waterfall in England. Did you know that?"

"Is it? And you're going to climb it?"

"Yes. And we climbed it last year. It's 180 metres long."

I looked down at him. It was impossible not to like him. Glasses, a mop of unruly hair, a desperate-thirst-for-knowledge expression.

"Do you go walking every year?"

I laughed. "No, this is our first year. And this is our fifth day. We finish tonight when we reach Dufton."

He nodded. "We're going home tomorrow."

"Where's home?" I said.

"Plymouth," he said.

"And then back to school?"

He smiled up at me. "I'm starting at the grammar school."

Where you'll be top of the class, I thought. But maybe with only one special friend. Socially awkward when girls appear on the radar.

I liked him a lot. I wanted to... What did I want? It would be years before Alex went walking with his son. I looked down at Stephen and realised I wanted to pass the father/son baton on to someone.

"Make sure you do this every year," I said. "And when you're older, just before you go to university, you should go off with your dad like we're doing. Make him promise. Better still, you promise me you'll take him every year."

"How will you know if I've kept my promise?"

"I won't. But I trust you."

Stephen beamed back at me. "You can trust me," he said. He put out his hand and as we walked by the side of the Tees, the sun shining down on us, we shook hands.

I turned around. His parents were laughing. "We made a deal," I said by way of explanation.

"That's good," his dad said. "Tell us about it while we have a cup of tea, Stephen."

"See you later," I said to him. "Lots of luck at your new school. And remember your promise."

They'd stopped at the right time. The path was gradually giving way to rocks.

"Are you going to be alright on these rocks, Dad?"

"For goodness sake, Alex, I've lived most of my life at the sea-side. Walking on rocks is second nature."

"Just take care. You're not the mountain goat you think you are."

I scoffed at my son's caution. What was there? 500 yards of rocks? Ten minutes' work. But they were awkward. Worn smooth – and slippery – by years of walkers. Angling sharply down to the black water of the river.

"You alright, Dad?"

"I'm fine. Only 50 yards to go. Then we'll have a cup of tea..."

Worn smooth. And *very* slippery...

My foot went from under me. I crashed down onto a large, flat rock. I didn't register any pain. But I was on my back, sliding headfirst towards the river. I flung my left hand out to stop myself going into the water. Or my head hitting a rock.

It worked. My hand crashed into another rock. I could feel water splashing across it. I lay still. Breathed out.

"Dad! Dad! Are you alright?"

I lay on my back and took stock. My back hurt. But not much. My legs were fine. Arms, shoulders... and most importantly, I hadn't hit my head. "I think I'm OK," I said. "Just let me lie here a minute. Get my breath back."

I tried to move myself around on the rock so I could sit up. Put my left hand out to give me some leverage. And the pain jolted straight up my arm. "Jesus," I said. "Christ, that hurts."

"What's the matter?"

"My hand. I used it to stop myself. Hell's bells..."

I couldn't spend the rest of the afternoon lying on a rock. Stupidly I found myself worrying about Stephen. They would have finished their tea by now. I didn't want him to come along and find me like this. "Give me your hand, Al. Help me up. Just do it gently."

I clambered unsteadily to my feet. Ran through the checklist again. Back, legs, arms, shoulders, head. All present and correct. Left hand, not good. It had stopped me going into the river, but it had taken all my weight: cut, grazed – and my ring finger and little finger were swelling up almost as I watched.

I made it to the end of the rocks. Found somewhere to sit down. "Ten minutes," I said. "Let's just have a cup of tea."

There was a patch of grass. I walked over to the river. Knelt down, put my left hand into the water. "What are you doing?"

"I'm holding my hand in the river. It's obvious. We've no ice so I'm holding it in cold water. It's what Bear Grylls would do."

Alex looked at me sadly. "Dad, Bear Grylls wouldn't have fallen over..."

"They wouldn't have shown it on TV, you mean."

I dried my hand. We sat down and had a cup of tea. I couldn't tear a sugar sachet open. "Al, can you just help me..."

And here was Stephen with his mum and dad.

"Hi again," I said.

Stephen grinned at me. "All good?" his dad asked.

"Never better. Just having a cup of tea before Cauldron Snout."

"Well, enjoy the climb."

"You too. Don't forget our deal, Stephen."

And they were gone. "Do you think you'll be able to do the climb, Dad?"

"Not much choice is there? Your mum can't drive the car down here. No mobile signal. Just us and the path." I finished my tea. "Let's go."

Alex picked up the backpack. Then he looked at me shrewdly. "You're going to exaggerate this aren't you?"

I smiled innocently at my son. He knew me too well. "Exaggerate it. Me?"

Footnote – or Fingernote

I didn't go to the hospital until a week later. A no-nonsense nurse delivered the verdict. "Good work, young man. Broken two fingers."

"Badly?"

"Awkwardly. Imagine your finger is hinged like a door. You've broken the hinge. Ring finger and little finger. We'll see you at fracture clinic on Tuesday morning."

Fracture clinic. Two appointments with orthopaedic surgeons. Exercises from the physio. Assorted splints. Nothing worked. So a year later I have a ring finger that won't bend properly, that's slightly misshapen. I can no longer make a fist with my left hand. A permanent reminder of the Pennine Way.

But let's look on the bright side. I was on my back, sliding head-first towards the rocks and the water. It's a small price to pay.

Besides, Alex was right. There's nothing a writer likes more than being a hero. And artistic licence. And time. Twenty years from now I shall have one of his children on my knee. As if I would exaggerate...

Tell me a story, Grandad.

I will, sweetheart. I'll tell you my favourite story. The one where I saved your daddy as we tumbled down a mountain towards a raging torrent. And then – you're not frightened are you, peanut – with my arm completely hanging off, how I carried your daddy through the wilderness to safety. Bears? Of course there were bears. Giant, ferocious, Teesdale bears...

At which point a grown-up, adult voice will break in. *That's enough now. Time for bed. And time for Grandad's medication. I think we may need to increase it...*

Cauldron Snout

"So we've got to climb up there?"

"Yeah. And then we turn left and walk along the top."

Sitting here, months later, writing the story, I realise how much I miss the Pennine Way. Sometimes you come back from holiday and you say, "It was fine. But I'm glad to be back." I'm not sure that I am. I'm not saying I want to repeat our five days – but I miss standing at the bottom of a hill with my son. I miss looking up and thinking, 'Hell's teeth, that's a steep hill. But I can do it. And I know I can do the hills that come after it as well.'

So I stood at the bottom of Cauldron Snout, told my throbbing fingers to be quiet and looked up at the longest waterfall in England. I knew I had to climb up the side of it. I knew I'd be scrambling and I knew I'd be frightened. I knew the chances were I was climbing it with a couple of broken fingers. But above all, I knew I didn't want these five days to end.

"Look," Alex said when we were half way up.

"What?"

"Over there." He pointed across the water. A rabbit was racing down the hill. It was being chased by a weasel. Yesterday my son sees a rabbit drop dead in front of him. Today he sees one torn apart by a weasel. Or maybe he doesn't. The rabbit suddenly veered left.

"Yeah. Go, rabbit!" Alex shouted.

The weasel couldn't turn that quickly: it was closer to going headlong into the Tees than it was to catching the rabbit. It slammed the brakes on just in time. The rabbit jogged confidently up the hill, easily living to fight another day.

...Which might be in doubt as far as I was concerned. We'd reached the point where scrambling was required: where two hands where definitely needed. I gritted my teeth and put my left hand out to support me. And realised that I didn't have the desperate need to lean into the hill I'd had on Pen y Ghent. That I'd left the Dementors behind me.

As we reached the top we saw Stephen and his parents sitting on a rock eating a sandwich. I waved at him. "Don't forget," I called.

"Promise," he shouted back.

And with that we turned left, leaving the bowl of Cow Green reservoir and heading west to Dufton. Three o'clock: eight miles to go by my reckoning. So let's say sixish. An hour late. I started to feel guilty. I couldn't imagine there was much to do in Dufton on a Friday evening.

This was probably the longest continuous climb of the whole week. Yes, it was a gravel road, so it should have been easy. But every time you thought you *had* to start coming down – "Back towards the river, Dad" – you'd turn a corner and there was another hill. Through Birkdale and up towards Moss Shop, through something marked 'danger area' on the map.

"What's that red flag, Dad?"

"It's nothing. Just means we're in the middle of a live firing range, that's all."

As if to confirm it a couple of low flying jets shot overhead. Maybe Vladimir Putin *had* been monitoring Yorkshire B&Bs after all...

Eventually we reached the top. "At last," I said. "And look, there's a sign down there. It should say, 'Dufton, 5 miles' if my maths is correct."

It wasn't. Eight miles. The guidebook I'd relied on had under-estimated again. Three extra miles. That was another hour.

"Mum's not going to be happy," Alex said.

"No. Let's hope there's something to do in Dufton." There was: if sitting in a car for three hours is your definition of 'something to do.'

"What time will we get there now?"

"Sevenish? Maybe home for ten. Seems like we had breakfast about four days ago."

There was nothing for it but to keep walking. We crossed the Tees for the final time and sat on the steps of the bridge to have our last cup of tea together. And finally, the fruit cake from Brunswick House. This was going to be a lot more than 20 miles: maybe 23 by the time we reached Dufton. Whatever was left, we ate it. If only we'd had some salt n' vinegar crisps...

High Cup Nick

A husband and wife were walking towards us. "Looks like we won't be the last people to see it tonight after all," he said. "You should just get there before the light fades."

It was only about six but he was right: the light *was* fading. Does the light fade more quickly when you're higher up? Or had we wandered into Scotland by mistake? I hadn't been in charge of the map so the second one was unlikely.

We tiptoed carefully through another stretch of boggy ground and there it was – a huge, stark slash cut in the Pennines, almost perfectly symmetrical, looking like a skateboard park for giants.

"Formed by glaciers," I said to Alex, showing off my limited knowledge of Geography for the final time.

I could have stayed at the top of High Cup Nick for a long time. I recommend you have your breakfast at the Tan Hill Inn – but if there's one sight I recommend from 'our' section of the Pennine Way, it's the first glimpse of High Cup Nick.

So yes, I could have stayed. But there was a wife and a mother waiting for her boys. And hopefully there was a first aid box waiting in her car, ideally containing a pain killer or three. My fingers were throbbing ominously.

So we began the long, gradual descent into Dufton. At first, the path took us along the edge of High Cup. On Monday I'd have been frightened of the drop. Now I was simply careful. Or maybe I was too tired to be frightened any more.

We were finally finished with walking uphill. It was, literally, all downhill from here. For half a mile or so the path was tricky: a couple of times when – painfully – I had to use my hands as well. But gradually the rocks gave way to grass, the path widened out. Any moment now and we'd see the village.

...And be in range of a phone signal. My mobile rang. I was so surprised I didn't realise what it was at first. My wife, ringing to see how much longer we'd be.

She'll read this and I don't want to phrase it wrongly. But at that moment I didn't want to talk to her. Alex and I were on the final lap. Metaphorically waving to the crowd. Five days when it had been just the two of us. I didn't want anyone else to intrude: I wanted to stay in my Pennine Way bubble with my son.

The path to Dufton was clearly marked, worn down by generations of walkers – but there were still piles of stones to mark the way. I stopped at one of them. "Hang on," I said to Alex, "I want to take a souvenir." I picked up a stone: one that would sit on my desk and remind me of the Pennine Way. I pushed it into a pocket and started down the hill again. Then I stopped. Did I seriously need a stone from the Pennine Way to remind me? Supposing everyone took a stone away? We were only visitors, here for five days. There would be countless people after us. The stones, and the Pennine Way, belonged to everyone – and the generations still to come.

I walk back and replace the stone. "Good move, Dad," Alex says.

"Hang on," I say to him. "I want to say this. Just in case I forget when we meet Mum. Thank you for coming with me. Thank you for giving me the chance to do this. Thank you. I love you."

"I love you too, Dad." And 2,000 feet above sea level, 5 days and nearly 90 miles behind us, we hug.

And no, we're not hugging at Everest base camp: it's not the end of a trek through the Andes. But for a middle-aged bloke who spent his life slumped over a keyboard and asked his son to go for a walk, it feels like it. This has been one of the best things I've ever done in my life – and I couldn't have done it without my son.

The End

And now here we are on a country lane. Up ahead of us a Land Rover pulls over and stops. Two sheepdogs leap out of the back. The door opens, the driver gets out.

"Evening," I say. "How far to the village?"

"Not far at all," he answers. "Ten minutes. Turn left, down the hill. Then turn right."

It's not even ten minutes. There's the sign. 'Dufton.' Population, not many. And nothing to do if you've been waiting three hours for a husband and a son. Yes, I feel guilty.

But we've arrived: we walk up the hill into the village, straight into the evening sun.

"Where is she?"

"By the village green? Just keep walking. We'll find her."

As we walk up the hill Alex starts to pull away from me. I'd imagined us walking into Dufton together, but he's in front and that seems right. I hang back and reflect on everything he's given me over the five days. Everything the Pennine Way has given me.

Memories that will last for the rest of my life: conquering my fears and climbing Pen y Ghent: the stunning moment when I stood at the top of High Cup Nick. If I'd known how hard the walk was going to be I would never have set off – but now all the ghosts I'd brought with me were buried, laid to rest on the moors and the fells.

There's the white car. We're done. Alex hugs his Mum. I kiss my wife. She gives us both a bottle of water. I walk over to a seat outside the post office. I unfasten my boots for the final time. "Thanks," I say to them. I walk back to the car – and then I pause.

Alex is in the car, demolishing sandwiches. I walk back up the road, and gaze towards High Cup Nick one final time. I close my eyes and replay the moment we hugged each other as we walked down from the summit.

Five days, nearly 90 miles, two broken fingers, a mile in my underpants and a lifetime of memories. And as I turn back to the car, I realise that Alex and the Pennine Way have given me one final gift. The wonderful certainty that sometime soon we'll lace up our boots again – and walk up a different hill, towards 'Father, Son and another five days...'

Part 3: Looking Back...
Things I Learned About My Dad on the Pennine Way...

"He can't read a map."

Beverley raised her eyebrows. "Tell me something I don't know. The only reason we're still married is the SatNav. Do you remember that time in France?"

"You mean when he got lost in the supermarket car park and you had the enormous argument?"

I'd hoped Alex had been too young to remember that little incident. Clearly not. They spent a happy couple of minutes reminiscing about my failings. "What else?" Bev asked.

"Well..."

We were talking about the Pennine Way over the dinner table. Alex and I had been back for a week and my wife – a psychologist – had put her professional hat on. "What did the experience teach you? What did you learn about your dad?"

But now Alex had scratched the couldn't-read-a-map itch, he could answer the question properly. Dad? He knows no fear: carries on when it's easier to quit: chats amicably to everyone he meets: oh, and he kept me amused for five days...

"Well..." my son said, "He can't *fold* a map either."

"No-one can fold an OS map," I said. But my protest fell on deaf ears.

"And he thinks grabbing on to a thistle for support is a good idea..."

"What?"

"We were between Hawes and Tan Hill. When it was raining. He slipped on a rock. To stop himself falling he grabbed hold of a thistle. Duh... And obviously he thinks he can change the weather by wearing shorts."

"He's always thought that. He thinks those disgusting blue ones have some sort of mystical power."

"He wore them every day. Even on Wednesday. It's pouring down and I've been woken up early by Dad watching 14 different weather forecasts. They all say the same. Rain and then more rain - "

"That's when he rang me up and had a hissy fit."

"Did he? I missed that. Damn. Anyway, everyone else is wearing their waterproofs. Dad looks out of the window and says it's easing up..."

"Was it?"

"Sure. It had eased from monsoon to downpour. So he sets off in his shorts, a t-shirt and his Ray Mears jacket."

My son shook his head sadly, but my wife was lapping it up. "Anything else?"

"Well, he can't spot a signpost – he walked straight past about six – but that goes hand in hand with map reading. He brags to strangers. Did you know that?"

Beverley just smirked.

"We met a few people on Wednesday – despite the rain. So we'd always ask them where they were going and they'd say, 'We're just doing a round trip, maybe five miles.' So Dad would sort of puff his chest out and say, 'Well we're walking from Hawes to Tan Hill.' And then he'd stand back and wait for a round of applause."

"Hang on a minute, darling. I'm enjoying this so much I need another gin and tonic."

"But the worst thing," Alex said when the glass was significantly more than half full, "Is that he told the same joke to every single person we met." At which my beloved very nearly snorted Bombay Sapphire down her nose.

"I've had that for twenty years!"

"Someone would say, 'When are you finishing?' and Dad would say – every single time – 'Friday. My wife's picking us up. Unless she's changed her mind about me over the last five days.'"

"And people would laugh?"

"Yes. That only encouraged him."

I coughed. It was time for someone to put a positive spin on events. "Took care of you," I said. "Shared my Kendal Mint Cake."

"Oh yeah," Alex said. "He did a really good job of stealing all the biscuits from the B&Bs..."

Things I learned about my son on the Pennine Way...

After Alex had finished his little homily I started thinking. What did I learn about my son on the Pennine Way?

Did I really learn anything? After all, I'd been his dad for nearly 18 years when we set off. And no, I don't think I did learn anything new – but I came to understand him more; to appreciate him on a deeper level.

I've written about why the challenge of the Pennine Way was so important to me. Alex instinctively understood that. He may not have understood the ghosts, my need to prove something to myself. He did understand that I *had* to finish. And he understood that I was way outside my comfort zone. He'd walked across a moor in the pouring rain. He'd walked in the Lake District and he'd hiked across the North York Moors – so Pen y Ghent and Great Shunner Fell didn't faze him: but he understood that they fazed me. And he allowed for that – and made sure we finished.

When Alex was in year 3 or 4 at school – so around 8 or 9 years old – he volunteered for the school cross-country team. At the time he wasn't a natural runner: 'stocky' is a kind way of putting it. A few years and he became a teenager: he shot up and the weight fell off. But back then he wasn't built for running. Never mind, the school was short – they needed four runners to make a team – and Alex volunteered. As dutiful parents, we went to watch.

He made no attempt to win. He wasn't remotely competitive. He knew his job for the team was simply to finish: to make sure the natural athletes were counted. So he jogged/walked round at the back chatting happily and encouraging the other kids who'd volunteered or been press-ganged into making up the numbers.

He made sure they finished: made sure they did their bit for their school. Ten years on he did his bit for *our* team: he simply made sure the other kid on the team finished the walk.

What else? He's tough. I staggered to the top of Pen y Ghent, told Alex I needed a photo of him and suddenly realised he'd carried the pack up 2,000 feet. But I didn't realise *how* tough until Wednesday: strong men would have given up that day. But he hauled the pack (literally) and his dad (figuratively) across the fells and the moors to Tan Hill.

Because he's like me in so many ways, he understood that the walk wasn't just about walking. He understood it was an internal journey for me as much as an external journey: that talking to Custard-and-Ice-Cream, breakfast at Tan Hill and saying 'thank you' as we walked down from High Cup Nick was every bit as important as reaching Dufton.

And he was funny. We kept each other amused. We were pals. He stole my joke, but I'll forgive him that...

Five days – all the statistics

So here we go. For the benefit of any Further Maths graduates who have made it to the end of the book, the statistics...

Total miles we walked: 87.55

Total time spent walking: 39 hours 18 minutes

Average speed: A blistering 2.23 mph

Shortest day: Horton to Hawes 13.62 miles

Longest day: Middleton to Dufton 23.77 miles

Number of blisters: None. Honestly, zero

Times we were hopelessly lost: 1

Bogs fallen into: 1

Miles walked in my underpants: 1.6

Times I felt like giving up: 2

Times I was physically frightened: 3

Steps taken on the Pennine Way: 199,061

Total steps, Monday to Friday: 212,205

Equivalent floors climbed: 1,325

Total ascent: 10,297 feet (3,138 metres)

Highest point: Great Shunner Fell 2,349 ft. (716m)

Lowest point: Looking out of the bedroom window on Wednesday morning and seeing the rain running down Hawes main street

Savage bites from savage insects: 5

Broken fingers (confirmed later): 2

Total rashers of bacon eaten: 37 (between us, obviously...)

And the day to day stats...

Monday: Malham to Horton-in-Ribblesdale

Distance: 15.62 miles

Steps taken: 35,654

Calories: 3,416

Ascent: 2,592 feet

Time: 6 hours 30 minutes

Tuesday: Horton to Hawes

Distance: 13.62 miles

Steps taken: 30,244

Calories: 2,799

Ascent: 1,364 feet

Time: 5:35

Wednesday: Hawes to the Tan Hill Inn

Distance: 16.95 miles

Steps taken: 40,470

Calories: 3,551

Ascent: 3,023 feet

Time: 8:29

Thursday: Tan Hill to Middleton-in-Teesdale

Distance: 17.59 miles

Steps taken: 39,372

Calories: 3,640

Ascent: 1,429 feet

Time: 7:36

Friday: Middleton to Dufton (via bog)

Distance: 23.77 miles

Steps taken: 53,321

Calories: 5,281

Ascent: 1,889 feet

Time: 11:08

Moving the Bags

Would someone really take our bags from one B&B to the next? Yes: there they were, nestled snugly in the hall.

It says a lot for my lack of preparation – for my spur of the moment request to Alex – that I'd given absolutely no thought at all to our bags. Clearly we couldn't carry everything. Cleary they needed moving from B&B number one to B&B number two.

I had no idea. Magic, possibly. Or maybe you stood in B&B number two, channelled your inner Harry Potter, and said 'Accio, toothbrush. And everything else that's in the bag.'

Or maybe people walked the Pennine Way pulling suitcases on wheels...

Not for the first time in the last 20 years my wife came to the rescue. "Someone at work did the Coast to Coast," she said. "A company moved their bags for them."

And there they were all over the internet. Google *Pennine Way bag transfer* and you'll be spoilt for choice.

We used Sherpa Van. They were absolutely fine, picking the bags up from River House as we headed towards Malham Cove and successively dropping them off in Horton, Hawes, Tan Hill and Middleton. The total cost for two bags was around £70.

But one word of caution if your initial planning is as ridiculous as mine: the baggage companies operate south to north on the

Pennine Way. My original plan had been to walk from north to south. Why? Because the sun rises in the east and sets in the west. I thought if we were walking south I'd get a nice tan. Which shows how pathetic my knowledge of walking was back in March.

The Cost

So what did it all cost?

Five nights in twin rooms in the B&Bs was £415. Twins rooms, five cooked breakfasts and – with one exception – a shower powerful enough to soothe away the aches and pains.

So yes, of course you can camp and that's a big, big saving. But there's simply no way I would have got through five days without a bed and a shower. 17 miles from Hawes to Tan Hill, soaked to the skin and then crawl into a tent? No, thank you.

Evening meals? Five again, averaging £25 a night. That was for fairly basic pub food and the world's worst curry. As I've already suggested, you don't walk the Pennine Way for the food.

Packed lunches; two at a fiver each, one – hopefully the subject of a Government enquiry – at £7.50. So £35 on packed lunches plus say another £15 spent in Hawes on pies, bread and cheese which lasted us for two days.

Purchases along the way – the flask and the map, both bought in Hawes. From memory they were about £28 – and if you're planning a few days' walking I'd seriously suggest spending one night in a town with shops. Or maybe you're just more experienced and more organised than I was. It wouldn't be difficult.

And now on to equipment: I doubt that any serious walkers have made it this far, but here's the embarrassingly slim list. A pair of waterproof trousers from Mountain Warehouse which, despite only costing £20, actually were waterproof. A couple of t-shirts – a tenner. One of the more sensible things I bought was a charger for my mobile: with the Walkmeter app running the battery only lasted until lunchtime, so I needed to charge the phone in the afternoon. Vital if you want to record the stats and available on Amazon for £12.

What about boots? Two pairs of good walking boots would have been expensive: Alex finished his Duke of Edinburgh practice expedition with his feet in plastic bags so we both needed boots.

As you know, our boots were sponsored. I approached two companies to see if they'd be interested in supplying us with boots in exchange for regular publicity through my blog and Hi-Tec came to the rescue. The boots were Altitude Pro RGS: I've just checked online and they're around £100. You can obviously spend far more on boots but they were great: yes, my feet got wet, but that was due to my own stupidity and lack of planning. And falling in a bog...

The boots were comfortable, they supported my ankles – absolutely crucial when you're walking over loose stones – and the blister count for the five days was nil.

Now we come to a surprising, but very welcome, gift that walking has given me: socks. I became obsessed with walking socks: not a sentence I ever thought I'd write. But never again will the family worry about what to buy me for Christmas. Nordic walking socks? Socks that cool your feet down? Socks that support your Achilles tendon? I'll have 'em all. Given that I bought a pair or two for Alex as well, add £50 for socks.

Finally to miscellaneous: plasters, mosquito repellent, anti-bite ointment. Probably £20 for the Mobile Army Surgical Hospital. And going back to March, the Ordnance Survey map which I helpfully left in the B&B at Middleham.

Add on £70 for Sherpa Van moving the bags and that's a grand total of around £800. So not the cheapest holiday in the world – but five days with my son? As the advert says, priceless...

The Awards

"We should have an awards ceremony," I said as we walked up the interminable hill from Cow Green Reservoir on the last afternoon.

"You mean like 'person who fell in the most bogs?' 'Person who missed the most signposts?'"

"No. You know, best breakfast - "

"This morning."

"OK. What else?"

"Best view? Funniest person we met?"

At that point we were distracted by realising we were walking through a live firing range. Then we were even more distracted by discovering we were three miles further from Dufton than we thought... and we never did get back to the awards.

But we've talked since. And for the benefit of anyone planning to follow in our footsteps or who simply wants a spectacular day out, here they are.

Best breakfast: while Louise gets an honourable mention for being one of the few women to truly understand me, this has to go to Brunswick House. If you book on the basis of breakfast, go there – and the room was lovely as well.

Best packed lunch: see above. By a Pennine Way mile.

Best view: I'm tempted to say the top of Pen y Ghent, if only because it meant I'd made it and wouldn't fall over the edge. But the real 'wow' moment was when I saw High Cup Nick. I remember turning a corner and seeing King's College, Cambridge for the first time. High Cup Nick had the same impact.

Funniest moment: very clearly, 'could I have a couple of poached eggs, please?' Although Alex will probably claim for his lightning wit as we left Brunswick House...

Most interesting person met en route: Everyone. That's not evading the question, it's simply a reflection of all the different people we met. Another failing on my part: I'd gone with preconceived ideas about walkers. The wide variety of people who were walking the Pennine Way was brilliant. There was dry wit, deep knowledge, genuine kindness, punk hairstyles and – on Wednesday – several raised eyebrows.

Best evening meal: technically, The Teesdale Hotel. But for the company, the sheer bloody relief at getting there and for custard and ice-cream with your pudding, 'best evening meal' goes to the Tan Hill Inn.

Moment I wanted to give up: there were two. On Wednesday I was walking along the paving stones on top of Great Shunner Fell. It was hailing, I was soaked, I could see about five yards either side of me in the fog and low cloud. Alex was ahead of me and I knew I was holding him back. And then the paving stones finished and I was back to wading up a stream. I had no idea how far we'd come or how far there was to go. But the worst thing was the reality of that endless, soaking slog: it was the complete opposite of everything I'd imagined. A very low moment...

...And so was breaking my fingers. If a helicopter had appeared there and then and lowered a ladder I'd have been tempted. Assuming I could have held on with one hand.

Best father/son moment: the conversation on the first morning when we said we'd do a walk every year? Making up after we'd fallen out? The best moment for me was saying 'thank you' to my son as we came down from High Cup Nick. We'd set out to do something, it had been far more difficult than we'd – alright, I'd – imagined: but we'd done it. And we'd done it together.

Most satisfying moment: the text-book answer is finishing. The 'dad answer' is watching my son stride up the hill into Dufton. The marriage guidance answer is seeing my wife again after five days...

Real ale drinkers will dismiss that touchy-feely nonsense out of hand. 'Nay lad. It were tha' first mouthful of Old Sheepdip Triple X after 17 miles in t' pouring rain.'

None of these is the answer. The most satisfying moment was starting. Taking the first few steps as we turned left out of the River House. Because that's when I knew we were actually doing it. That's when I knew I'd made a commitment to myself and kept it. That's when six months and all the miles of training was worth it.

That's when it was father and son: just the two of us against whatever nature – and the Pennine Way – had in store for us. As you now know, I had no idea of what *was* coming, but setting off with my son was a perfect moment.

What I'd do differently

It's easy to say I should have been fitter but, given the limits imposed by work and family commitments, on August 1st I was as fit as I could be. The big mistake I made was not training with a backpack. Tuesday morning was the first time in my life I'd walked with a backpack and I was totally unprepared for it – for the way it changes your centre of gravity and for just how heavy the damn thing is. There was, though, one silver lining: whatever the pack weighed, it was less than the weight I'd lost through walking.

I'd spend more time reading the map the night before. Yes, yes, I know. The only time I studied the map the night before I came out of the B&B and turned left instead of right. But next time it'll be different...

And somehow reading the OS map gives you a *feel* for the walk: you start to establish a connection with the countryside you're going to walk through. I've come to love looking at OS maps. At school they were just another stick to beat you with – "How many times, boy? It's a church with a spire" – but as an adult I think they're rather beautiful.

OS maps appeal to the traditionalist in me: that said, I'd still make sure I had them all on my phone. Much easier to fold...

I'd write times on the map: we should be here at 11 o'clock. And about here by salt n' vinegar crisp time. That, I think might have stopped our navigational cock-up on the last day. But then I'd never have fallen in the bog and become one of the very few people in the world to walk a section of the Pennine Way in his underpants.

I emphatically would not 'draw a line through waterproof jacket for Dad.' I'd underline it. About eight times.

And obviously, I'd make sure we took two backpacks: which sadly brings me back to training...

31ˢᵗ March 2006

'Ten years ago – completely out of the blue – I was critically ill.'

That's what I wrote at the beginning of the book. I didn't want to spoil the flow of the story with 1,000 words of medical details. But I think they're important in understanding why the Pennine Way meant so much to me. Here's the full story...

March 31ˢᵗ is my birthday, so it's always a memorable day. March 31ˢᵗ 2006 was just a tad more memorable.

It was a Friday. I worked in the morning and then met my wife for lunch: the bistro at the Stephen Joseph Theatre in Scarborough. I had liver and bacon, because I hadn't had liver and bacon for years. Eleanor was ten at the time, starring as Little Miss Fussy. The chance of liver and bacon at home wasn't even zero.

We finished the wine and looked at each other. It was about one-thirty. "Anything urgent this afternoon?" I said.

"Not really..."

"The kids don't need collecting until four. Let's go home."

When your children are 12, 10 and 7 you don't get too many chances to have sex in the afternoon. Or in the morning or evening, come to that. We weren't going to waste one. Besides, it was my birthday. I may have driven through a red light in my excitement...

"That was lovely," I said. And then I rolled over and lay on my back. And then I rolled over again, onto my right side.

"Are you OK?"

"I think so. I don't know. I just feel a bit odd."

"Indigestion, darling. Or maybe you're getting old..."

I didn't reply to my wife's jibe, which wasn't a good sign. "I'm going to the bathroom," I said.

By the time I reached the bathroom I was in pain. If this was indigestion it was like no indigestion I'd ever felt before. Jesus Christ it hurt. I got down on my hands and knees. "Bev," I called – and fell over on my side, slumped against the bath.

"What - " Bev stopped short. "Bloody hell, you don't look well."

"I don't feel well. Pain. In my chest. Like a steel ball."

"You don't think - "

"Yes, I do," I said. "I think I'm having a heart attack."

I tried to get back on my knees. But the steel ball was still expanding. I was cold. I was clammy. More than that, I was frightened.

"I'll phone an ambulance."

"No," I said, "Put me in the car. Drive me to A&E. Please..." I added. "Will you dress me?"

Somehow I made it into some clothes. Made it downstairs and into the car. We only live five minutes from the hospital. Six if you stop at the red lights. "Drive straight through them," I said.

Somehow I staggered to the reception desk. Told them I'd had a heart attack. Collapsed onto a chair.

Then I was on a bed. Leads and wires being attached. Equipment wheeled in. Graphs flickering. Consultants arriving.

"Take him through," one of them said.

The bed moved. Into another room. I looked around desperately for Bev. Reached out to hold her hand.

And then suddenly I was watching. A middle aged bloke on a bed. He hadn't brushed his hair. One of his socks was inside out. What was happening? A doctor was fixing pads to his chest.

I'd seen this before. On *Casualty*. They fixed the pads, then they shouted "Charging! Stand clear!" and then they shocked the poor bugger. Sometimes it worked: sometimes it didn't. Not good. And watching wasn't good. Any minute now there'd be a bright light: Mum and Dad would be waiting for me...

I forced myself back on to the bed. Someone was talking to me.

"Can we just check your date of birth?"

"March 31st," I said.

"That's today," a voice said. I looked to my right. A junior doctor. Long blonde hair. Yellow jumper. Not wearing a white coat. "Happy birthday," she said.

"Maybe not," I said. "But thank you."

She turned around to write something down.

Blimey, I thought, she's got a nice bum.

So, Junior Doctor, who by the law of averages is now qualified, married and quite possibly with children of your own, thank you. The moment you turned around and I looked at your bum was the moment I knew I wasn't going to die.

Gradually they removed the pads. I was wheeled down to the heart unit. Down a long and remarkably bumpy corridor. "Hang on," I said to the porter. "I'm going to be sick."

He passed me one of those cardboard top hats the NHS uses for collecting vomit.

"Impressive," he said when I'd finished.

"Liver and bacon," I said.

I was in hospital for four days. They let me go home when I could walk up a flight of stairs. I fell into bed and watched a Champions League game on ITV. 'Tomorrow morning,' I said to myself. 'Tomorrow morning I start to get fit again.'

How had it happened? How could someone who played football with his boys and ran with his daughter have a heart attack? How could I have a heart attack out of the blue with no warning signs?

Over the weeks that followed I Googled *fit people, sudden heart attack* a lot. I knew it had happened to footballers: but it wasn't just footballers. There were stories from all over the world. Most of them ending in tragedy. How had my body – that had run four half-marathons – let me down so badly?

The simple fact was, it had. Whatever the reason, I had to put it right.

So my first target was simple: to walk to the lamppost nearest our house.

And on that Wednesday morning in April 2006 I couldn't do it.

That moment – the moment I looked up and saw the lamppost and realised I couldn't reach it – had haunted me for ten years. And so had the expression on Dan's face.

But in ten years things slip. You become complacent; start to take your health for granted again. You have an extra slice of toast, you sit at your desk all day, you don't exercise enough. I'd become unfit and overweight.

I needed to do something. I needed to prove I was still alive, if only to myself. And once and for all, I needed to lay my ghosts to rest.

80 miles in five days seemed a reasonable way of doing that. And that's why the challenge of the Pennine Way was so important to me. That, and spending time with my son.

Final Thoughts

I miss the Pennine Way. I'm writing these final paragraphs in early autumn: it's a beautiful, crisp, clear morning. I've just walked five miles on the cliff top with Pepper – the Cleveland Way, where I first started my training.

But what I really want to do on a crisp, clear autumn morning is walk from Hawes to Tan Hill. That's the one day I want to repeat. I want to look at the map and set off from Hawes on a dry, sunny morning so I can see what we achieved. I want to enjoy the views we missed – and test myself again.

But the rest of the 87 miles? No. It was a one-off. I don't want to spoil the memories. As long as I live I want to keep the image of Alex walking up the hill into Dufton and the setting sun...

I started this book by saying I wanted it to be an inspiration: let me end it the same way. Being a dad has been the great joy of my life – and our five days on the Pennine Way summed it up perfectly.

Parenting doesn't always go according to plan. You'll make mistakes and occasionally you'll lose your way. Sometimes you'll fall out. But if you take the journey *with* your children then ultimately – like the moment we set off, like Tan Hill emerging from the mist, like standing together at the top of High Cup Nick – it will be wonderful.

About me

Way back in 2003 I was at a meeting of the local writers' circle. The speaker was the editor of the local paper who said, "We'd quite like a humorous weekly column if anyone thinks they can write one." That was the start of writing about my family: something I've done every week for 14 years, beginning when Alex was four.

We've gone from party bags, nativity plays and the sheer hell that's a family changing room at the swimming pool, to teenage angst, slamming doors and – ultimately – leaving home. You can read some of the columns online at www.bestdadicanbe.com and – as you'll see below – they'll shortly all be published in book form.

I was voted the UK's 'Funniest Dad Blogger' and the blog has consistently been ranked in the UK's top 3 humour blogs and in the top 100 worldwide.

At the time I started writing I worked in financial services, but in 2009 my brother died from cancer. It was one of those pivotal moments in life, and six months later I sold my business to do what I'd always wanted to do: write full time. I now work as a copywriter, speech-writer and ghost-writer.

And as you now know, early in 2016 I suffered the latest in a long list of mid-life crises and invited my youngest son to come for a walk with me...

You can connect with me online at:

W - www.markrichards.co.uk

T - @BestDadICanBe

F - https://www.facebook.com/MarkRichardsAuthor/

Future Writing Plans

Thank you for reading *Father, Son and the Pennine Way*. I really hope you enjoyed it.

If you did, could I ask a favour? Would you please review the book on Amazon? Reviews are important to me for three reasons: first of all, good reviews help to sell the book. Secondly, there are some review and book promotion sites that will only look at a book if it has a certain number of reviews and/or a certain ratio of 5* reviews. Lastly, reviews are feedback: these 40,000 words took a lot of writing – and I'd value your honest opinion. So I'd really appreciate you taking five minutes to leave a review, and thank you in advance to anyone who does so.

What next?

The immediate aim has to be publicity for 'Pennine Way.' Writing a book is only half the battle: publicising it is every bit as important and, as an independent author, that will be down to me. In production terms I now have the paperback and the e-book published: I'll also be looking into the possibility of doing an audiobook of 'Pennine Way.'

And then – as you've seen from the 'About Me' section – my intention is to publish my full series of 'Best Dad' books, covering 14 years and more than 400,000 words of family life. There will be seven books in total, all published by the summer of 2018. If you'd like a sneak preview, there is a sample book available on Amazon: just search Mark Richards: Best Dad I Can Be.

...And somewhere in the middle of all that look out for another, 'Father, Son and...' book. Yes, Alex and I are planning another trip for the summer of 2018. We're not sure where yet, but 'don't fall in another bog' is high on the list of priorities...

When all that's done I'll be moving on to novels. Right now I'm playing God: creating characters, working out plots and deciding who lives and who falls 300 feet into the icy waters of the North Sea...

If you'd like to receive regular updates on my writing, including previews, short stories and exclusive content, simply drop me an e-mail and I'll add you to my mailing list.

Join the team

Writing is a lonely business: sometimes you need friends. Specifically, what every writer needs are comments, suggestions, thoughts and feedback: someone to say, 'that part of the book is really interesting – you need to develop it more.' Or – more probably – 'that section didn't add anything to the story. Is it really necessary?'

I'm now starting to build a team of people who'll give me exactly that feedback. I'll send them samples of books, plot ideas and thoughts on potential characters: they will (hopefully) come back and say, 'Have you thought about developing the plot in this way?' 'Supposing the main character did that instead...'

If you'd like to join my team, I'd be delighted to hear from you: my e-mail address is mark@markrichards.co.uk

You'll get an insight into the mind of a working writer, and you'll play a direct part in influencing the shape of future books – especially the novels. You'll also earn my undying thanks...

We Should Talk About This...

"We should talk about this," I said as we continued our serene progress along the river bank.

Well, we're back, and we're available. Alex and I will be more than happy to talk about 'Father, Son and the Pennine Way' if you'd like a different type of speaker for your business, club, society or for after dinner.

Since he was persuaded to give the vote of thanks as a 14 year old, Alex went on to twice lead his school team to the national finals of the 'Youth Speaks' competition, both times being voted Best Speaker in the North of England.

So if you'd like to be entertained and amused by probably the only father/son public speaking duo in the country, drop me an e-mail: mark@markrichards.co.uk

Acknowledgements

There are a number of people to thank, starting with someone I've never met. My thanks to Kevin Partner, for all his technical help. Look forward to working with you for a long time to come, Kev.

Many people have helped with the proof-reading and made suggestions on content: thank you to all of them. But some of the very best insights and suggestions came from my daughter, Eleanor. Thanks for your help, darling – don't outsell me too quickly.

I'd also like to say thank you to the Walk1,000Miles group on Facebook, whose comments, support, encouragement, correction of mistakes and – in one case – determined research has been beyond helpful. Thank you all.

And to my own writing group on Facebook – again, people I've never met. Thanks for all your input and constructive criticism: here's to a good few years together...

Printed in Great Britain
by Amazon